Eleven Vests & T

Two plays for young people on the devastating effects of war and violence.

Eleven Vests

Two events involving the same person – in the first as a young teenager, in the second years later as an adult. They are strangely alike but at the same time worlds apart. It's as if the first event were turned upside down by the second. Partly this is because teenagers must answer to authority but adults must first answer to themselves. *Eleven Vests* shows how the adult self develops out of the earlier self. It asks: how do we learn responsibility for ourselves and what we do?

Tuesday

A young girl sits alone in her bedroom studying for exams. Her soldier boyfriend arrives unexpectedly from active service abroad. What happens in the little room during the next ninety minutes changes the girl for ever: her attitude to her father, war and violence, and life itself.

Edward Bond was born and educated in London. His plays include *The Pope's Wedding* (Royal Court Theatre, 1962), *Saved* (Royal Court, 1965), *Early Morning* (Royal Court, 1968), *Narrow Road to the Deep North* (Belgrade Theatre, Coventry, 1968; Royal Court, 1969), *Black Mass* (Sharpeville Commemoration Evening, Lyceum Theatre, 1970), *Passion* (CND Rally, Alexandra Palace, 1971), *Lear* (Royal Court, 1971), *The Sea* (Royal Court, 1973), *Bingo* (Northcott, Exeter, 1973; Royal Court, 1974), *The Fool* (Royal Court, 1975), *The Bundle* (RSC Warehouse, 1978), *The Woman* (National Theatre, 1978), *The Worlds* (New Half Moon Theatre, London, 1981), *Restoration* (Royal Court, 1981), *Summer* (National Theatre, 1982), *Derek* (RSC Youth Festival, The Other Place, Stratford-upon-Avon, 1982), *The Cat* (produced in Germany as *The English Cat* by the Stuttgart Opera, 1983), *Human Cannon* (Quantum Theatre, Manchester, 1986), *The War Plays* (*Red Black and Ignorant*, *The Tin Can People* and *Great Peace*), which were staged as a trilogy by the RSC at the Barbican Pit in 1985, *Jackets* (Leicester, Haymarket, 1989), *September* (Canterbury Cathedral, 1989), *In the Company of Men* (Paris, 1992; RSC at the Barbican Pit, 1996), *At the Inland Sea* (toured by Big Brum Theatre-in-Education, 1995); *Eleven Vests* (toured by Big Brum Theatre-in-Education, 1997); *Olly's Prison* (BBC2 Television, 1993), *Tuesday* (BBC Schools TV, 1993). His *Theatre Poems and Songs* were published in 1978, *Poems 1978–1985* in 1987, and his recent play *Coffee* in 1995.

Edward Bond

ELEVEN VESTS
&
TUESDAY

with full teaching notes and an interview with the author by
Jim Mulligan

Methuen Drama

Methuen Modern Plays

The right of Edward Bond to be identified as the author of this work has been
asserted by him in accordance with the Copyright, Designs and Patents Act, 1988

This volume first published in Great Britain in 1997
by Methuen
Random House, 20 Vauxhall Bridge Road, London SW1V 2SA

Random House Australia (Pty) Limited
20 Alfred Street, Milsons Point, Sydney, New South Wales 2061, Australia

Random House New Zealand Limited
18 Poland Road, Glenfield, Auckland 10, New Zealand

Random House South Africa (Pty) Limited
Endulini, 5A Jubilee Road, Parktown 2193, South Africa

Random House UK Limited Reg. No. 954009

Distributed in the United States of America
by Heinemann, a division of Reed Elsevier Inc.
361 Hanover Street, Portsmouth, New Hampshire NH 03901 3959

A CIP catalogue record for this book is available from the British Library

Papers used by Random House UK Limited are natural, recyclable products made
from wood grown in sustainable forests. The manufacturing processes conform to
the environmental regulations of the country of origin.

ISBN 0 413 72120 5

Typeset by Deltatype Ltd, Birkenhead, Merseyside
Printed and bound in Great Britain by Cox & Wyman Ltd, Reading, Berkshire

Contents

Eleven Vests

Eleven Vests was first presented by Big Brum on 7 October 1997 in Birmingham, prior to a tour of the Midlands. The company comprised Bobby Colvill, Mandy Finney and Chris Cooper (actor/teachers); Geoff Gillham, director; Richard Watson, designer.

Characters

Student
Head
Other Student
Weapons Instructor
Soldier
Enemy Soldier
Prisoner
Voices of Prisoners and Students

Note

Eleven Vests is a play for three or more actors in seven scenes.

Scenes

Book
Jacket
Gate
Lesson
Reccy
Roof
Tower

Book

*The **Head** questions the **Student**.*

Head   Why? D'you know why? What did you gain by it?
Answer me. Do you deny it's your handiwork? Well? I
didn't see you do it. No one did. I accuse you because I
know none of my other pupils would do it. It has your
trademark all over it. And you did it on your own. You
couldn't involve anyone else. The others wouldn't be so
stupid. Aren't you going to speak? I shall take your silence
as a confession of guilt. Well? Thank you for not wasting
my time with fatuous denials. At least you spare me that.
Not that you lack the effrontery to deny it and let the
blame fall on some innocent person. A selfish disregard for
the well-being of others. Only you're too clever to try. Yes
that made you look at me! You know you wouldn't get
away with it. Why did you do it? I'd like an explanation –
or at least an excuse. Take your time. I can wait.

Head *takes out a book with slashed pages.*

Head   Destruction for destruction's sake. Take it. Are you
ashamed to hold it in your hands?

*The **Head** tries to give the **Student** the book. The **Student***
*refuses it. The **Head** wedges a corner of the book in the **Student**'s*
pocket and steps back. The book falls to the ground.

Head   D'you want to be expelled? Don't look out of the
window when I talk to you. Don't look on the ground. I
suppose you think this silence makes you tough? You don't
have to conform because you're special? Too good for us!
You're not. I've seen them standing where you are – the
no-hopers, the non-achievers. I see you five years from
now. I read you like this book – only it makes more sense
than you do even in the dilapidated state you've reduced it
to. Some of our young people respect books. They want to
learn. Now I shall have to lock the library room when it's
unattended. Would-be readers will have to come to my
secretary for the key. So everyone is punished because of
you. You're not stepping out of this room till you say

something. D'you think I like questioning you? Exercising
my power? I have better things to waste my time on. I get
no satisfaction from knocking my head on a brick wall. I
do it so that you can't tell yourself you had no chance.
You're not going to deceive yourself on that! You're given
every chance. Are you going to speak? I try to help you
because you can't help yourself. Pick up the book and tell
me why you vandalised it. Then we'll forget about it. I
don't have to report it to the governors. We'll throw it in
the bin and you can go back to your class. My secretary
will find out what it cost. You will pay for it in instalments.
We'll set a weekly sum you can afford. Our parents have
to work to buy books for the school. I suppose that doesn't
concern you? You won't get a job – you won't try – so
you'll never be asked to pay for anything. Pick it up. It
makes no difference to me what you do. It makes a great
deal of difference to me when school property is destroyed.
I did concern myself with you once. When you entered this
school with your intake I had hopes for all of you. I didn't
make the world what it is. I hoped I could help you and
the others to survive in it. I even hoped that when the time
came for you to leave some of you would go out and make
it a better place. That's why I became a teacher. There! –
I've confessed something to you about my life. Can't you
confess about a *book*? Just say you regret what you've done.
You don't even have to mean it. Just make the gesture to
what decent civilised people do. Then we have a
foundation to build a relationship on. It's only a book.
You're worth more than a book. Tell me something: don't
you want to be happy? I don't think you do. It's too
simple. You don't know why you destroyed the book. You
don't know why you do anything. It's not just me you can't
talk to. You can't talk to yourself. That's why you'll destroy
yourself. If this were a story you'd end up running the
school library. Life isn't like that. It's like this book. I can't
spare you any more time. I have things to attend to. Other
pupils have needs. I shall write to your parents. If you
commit any further nuisance you will be expelled. This is

the final warning. I shall have to put you down as one of my failures. Please close the door as you go.

*The **Head** watches the **Student** go and then picks up the book and goes in the opposite direction.*

Jacket

__Other Student__ comes in crying and carrying a jacket.

Other Student Miss. Miss. (*No one comes.*) Miss.

*The **Head** comes in.*

Head What is the matter?

Other Student I was looking for Miss Tyler.

Head Why are you crying? Its no use crying if you can't tell me why. Don't be a silly. I'm sure it's not as bad as you think.

*The **Other Student** gives the **Head** a jacket. The **Head** unfolds it. It has been slashed.*

Head When was this done?

Other Student I found it.

Head In the cloakroom?

Other Student My mum'll –

Head Did you see who did it?

Other Student I'll get into trouble when I go home. My mum'll say it's my fault. I must've done something to deserve it. I didn't, I didn't.

Head Was anything stolen?

Other Student It's my new jacket.

Head Did you leave anything in the pockets? We have a rule against leaving things in pockets in cloakrooms.

Other Student   No.

Head   Have you looked? Crying won't help us. Are you sure you left nothing in them? (*Looks in the pockets. They are empty.*) Can you think of who would do such a thing? Have you quarrelled with anyone?

Other Student   My mum'll say I didn't take proper care of –

Head   Has anyone in the school threatened you? You know the school policy on bullying. If you're being bullied you should report it straight away to a senior member of staff. Then we can stop it getting out of hand so that things like this happen. Stop those tears. You're not a child any more. Don't be afraid to speak. We'll look after you. Think before you answer. Other people's happiness will depend on what you say. This is beyond a practical joke. It's a serious matter.

Other Student   My mum'll –

Head   I'll write to her and say it's not your fault.

Other Student   She said I didn't deserve a new jacket because I didn't know how to look after it. She says I never take proper care of anything. It's new this week. My old jacket's too small. I'll have to wear it again.

Head   Put this on. (*The* **Other Student** *stares at the* **Head**.) Put on the jacket.

Other Student   I can't.

Head   Yes you can.

Other Student   It's all cut.

Head   I know what I'm doing. Put it on.

Other Student   No.

Head (*going to the* **Other Student**)   I'll help you. Let me deal with this my way.

The **Head** *helps the* **Other Student** *into the jacket.*

Other Student   I don't want it. I don't want it.

Head   Try not to cry. Have you a hanky or tissues? Dry your face. (*Turns to go.*) Fasten the buttons.

The **Head** *goes out. The* **Other Student** *stands in the jacket trying to poke the lining back inside the cuts. Gives up. The* **Head** *returns with the* **Student**.

Head (*to the* **Student**)   Is this what you wanted? Why? I'd like to understand. We'd both be interested.

The **Other Student** *starts to cry again.*

Head   Don't give him the satisfaction of tears. I'm partly to blame. I might as well have driven you to it! I thought I could help you. Vanity! – as if I could change the world. I should have known better than to give you another chance. You were bound to turn my kindness against me and treat it as a challenge. (*To the* **Other Student**.) Don't cry. You'll come across his type all through your life. Get to know them so you can avoid them. (*To the* **Student**.) Why *this* jacket? Was it the first you came to? Was it because you haven't got a new jacket?

Other Student (*to the* **Student**)   My mum'll row me when I –

Head   Don't talk to him. He must be isolated from the rest of us while he's in the building. (*To the* **Student**.) I can't allow you to remain in the school. The governors would certainly override any leniency I showed you. The other children's parents would demonstrate at the school gates. You'll be expelled – which I assume is what you want. Unfortunately it can't end there. You've committed criminal damage. I'm sorry for your parents. My secretary's called the police –

Other Student   No please!

Head   Hush.

Other Student   My mum'll blame me for –

Head   I told you I'll write to your mother. (*To the* **Student**.) If I failed in my legal obligation to report the matter and you went on to do – heaven knows what!: which you would – this affair with the jacket today – it would all come out. I can't risk an embarrassment to the governors. You're not worth it. For once in your life be sensible and listen to me. (*To the* **Other Student**.) Do be quiet! (*To the* **Student**.) There's still a little time left. Explanations and excuses will be too late when the police are here. They won't have time to listen, they have to look after prisons full of people like you. Tell me why you did it. It doesn't have to make sense. At least it would be something to talk about. (*The* **Other Student** *starts to take off the jacket*.) Leave it for a moment. Keep it on.

Other Student   I don't want it.

The **Other Student** *stands with one arm out of its sleeve*.

Head (*to the* **Student**)   Am I an ogre? Is it my fault? Or someone else's? Have I wrongly accused you? Did you do it? You can't go on doing these things. What will it be next? Talk to me. The times I've asked you! Does it have to be so difficult? We stand here – two sensible people. Surely we can help each other? You're not wicked. If you showed some contrition . . . It's such a shame. The book, the jacket, your life – all wasted. It makes me angry. Empty your pockets.

The **Student** *does not move. The* **Head** *goes to him and searches his pockets. There is nothing incriminating in them*.

Head   Obviously you got rid of it. To use again? What did you hope to gain? You knew you'd be found out.

The **Head** *produces the slashed book*.

Head   These pages and the jacket are of different materials. But even an untrained eye can see both were cut with the same instrument. The police won't need a forensic scientist to tell them that.

Other Student Can I take it off now? He's not going to —

Head Use your tissue. D'you feel able to go straight back into class? It's best if you can. Concentration helps us to settle down. That's better. Now you look your normal self. You don't want to go into class showing everyone you've been crying. It's History Three isn't it? Tell your teacher I'll be along to have a word with her.

The **Other Student** *starts taking off the jacket.*

Head You're not to do it. Let him help you. (*To the* **Student**.) You did the damage. Now clear up the mess.

The **Student** *goes to the* **Other Student**.

Head I see you cut out the school badge.

The **Student** *rips strips from the jacket. The* **Other Student** *backs away.*

Other Student Don't! Don't!

Head (*to the* **Student**) What a little coward we are!

The **Other Student** *takes off the jacket and throws it on the floor.*

Head (*to the* **Other Student**) Go to my office. Tell my secretary I said you were to wait for me. She'll find you a quiet corner. I'll be there shortly.

The **Other Student** *goes out.*

Head The world's your playground. You do what you like in it. What'll you do when you meet a —

The **Student** *goes out.*

Head (*calling*) You will wait here with me for the police!

The **Head** *picks up the jacket and torn strips and goes out after the* **Student**.

Gate

The **Other Student** *leaves the school through the gate. The* **Student** *comes along the street. They stop and look at each other. The* **Student** *passes the* **Other Student** *and goes to the gate. He looks into the school yard.*

Other Student   Do the police know you're here? You'll be seen standing there. They've got cameras to watch the gates. Why've you come back? I'm sorry I made the fuss. I was upset. I didn't have time to think. I could've got rid of it and said I'd lost it on the bus. I don't care what they say. Let them row. I get blamed anyway. If it wasn't the jacket they'd think of something else. Your photo was in the local paper. You're famous. A missing person. I cut it out. You've been living on the streets. Where d'you sleep? Isn't it cold? At least there's no one to shout at you.

The **Student** *moves from the gates but still looks into the yard.*

Other Student   You upset them. I have to tell them everything now. What I do. Where I've been. Who I saw. They keep asking me why you did it to the book and the jacket. I know why. It's obvious. If they don't know that how can they teach us anything? Sometimes I want to smash all the windows in the street. One day I might walk out and never come back. Then mum'll sit in my room and cry. Too late. She'll never see me again. Gran says you didn't smack that child hard enough when it was a tot that's what's wrong. Sometimes I'd like to smack her. Pull her blue rinse out by the roots. Don't stand there. They'll call the police. Let's walk down the canal.

The **Head** *comes on behind the* **Other Student***'s back.*

Head   Good morning. What is it you want? (*To the* **Other Student**.) Did he waylay you as you left school? Has he threatened you? (*To the* **Student**.) Aren't you ashamed of all the trouble you cause? (*To the* **Other Student**.) Go back into school. (*The* **Other Student** *does not move.*) Go inside. I don't want you here.

The **Other Student** *goes inside the gate but stops to watch.*

Head   Have you been home? You haven't contacted your mother for three months. If you didn't want to come back you could have phoned so that she knew you were alive. I had a long talk with her. I can see she's not an easy woman to live with. You have to be patient. Instead you've made her ill. She has to take tranquillisers. (*Sees the* **Other Student**.) Go inside the building. (*The* **Other Student** *does not move.*) O for heaven's sake! (*To the* **Student**.) Wherever you are there's trouble. What d'you want standing there? You must want something. Have you been drinking? Or is it drugs? (*To the* **Other Student**.) I order you to go inside.

The **Other Student** *goes out.*

Head   You're not going inside. You're a trespasser. The students are forbidden to have anything to do with you – even if they'd wanted to. If you can't behave as a normal member of society you must stay with your own kind. Decent people will shun you. I wanted to help you but you refused. You're no longer my responsibility. But I'll stand by you. I won't cast you off. The governors can't readmit you to the school. But I can talk to the police on your behalf. May I? I'm not your head now so you can talk to me as an equal. Why do you do these things? Is the rest of the world wrong and you the only one in the right? You're not going through the gate.

The **Other Student** *comes to the gates.*

Other Student   Run! The police are coming.

Head (*to the* **Other Student**)   Go inside!   *Female*

Other Student   Her secretary phoned them. She's talking to keep you till they get here.

Head (*to the* **Other Student**)   Stop this nonsense at once! Inside! – d'you hear? I'll deal with you later.

Other Student   Run!

Head   Of course we called the police. You can't manage!

We have to protect you from yourself! Where've you been
for three months? You come here and silly little people –
(*Gesture to the* **Other Student**.) like this – think it's an
exciting adventure. You waste your youth. You catch
diseases. You're undernourished. In a few years you'll be
old. And then you're dead. And who will mourn you? I will
not have you come here – with your stupid, arrogant little
posturings – and lead my wards astray! It's so easy! You
drop out and think you've accomplished something clever.
No effort, no work. The others have to make the effort to
work and earn – and you're a parasite on them. Why
d'you stand there and glare? The little ones will see you.
You'll frighten them. Aren't you ashamed? (*To the* **Other
Student**.) Is that what you want? – live on the streets with
him? You'll soon find if it's an adventure! You make me
angry. I stand here – with my profession – the values I've
lived by and taught – to defend them against a little rough
– a little tough – who's come to drag us down to his state
of barbarism!

Other Student   Run!

Head   Tell this silly child why you're here. You can't! (*To
the* **Other Student**.) Your friend doesn't know!

Other Student   Why don't you run? You're getting me
into more trouble!

Head   That won't worry him. At least what he does is in
the open. You've deceived me behind my back. I wouldn't
have believed you had such slyness in you. You shame your
parents and disgrace the school.

Other Student (*to the* **Student**)   Please go!

Head   Inside the building!

Other Student   No!

Head   Inside! You're still under my jurisdiction in school
hours!

Other Student   I'm not! I'm not! Miss Tyler dismissed
me early to do my project work.

*The **Other Student** goes out down the street. The **Head** stands in the gateway facing the **Student**.*

Head You're not coming in. Some rules are not broken. I'm not a child you can frighten. Or a fool who thinks it's clever – original – to have a knife. By mischance some of the little ones saw the coat after you'd destroyed it. Can you imagine what they felt? What dreams they had? One dreamt of animals being cut and hacked. The whole school was in turmoil. I had to quieten them in assembly. I will not put them through that ordeal again. How can they study when they're disturbed? *(Glances back.)* Look the children are watching us from every window. I will not be defied by you in front of their young faces. What lesson would that teach them? To give way to brutes? Why d'you stand there and glare? You look so menacing. Are you ill? *(Calls.)* Miss Ampton! *(To the **Student**.)* You won't get away with it. You're not skulking in a cloakroom now. There are all these witnesses. You've overstepped the mark! *(Calls.)* Miss Ampton send the caretaker to me! *(To the **Student**.)* You will not pass through this gate.

Other Student *(off. Calls)* Don't argue with him Miss! Please come away! It only makes trouble!

Head *(to the **Other Student**)* Go to the corner and wait for the police. *(To the **Student**.)* I shall not let you pass. *(Calls.)* Miss Ampton send the caretaker with the keys to lock the gate!

Other Student *(off. Calls)* Please! Please! Leave him there!

Head You can't get into the school building. The doors are locked. You'd stand in the middle of the playground and glare. How silly you'd look! Even the little ones would laugh.

Other Student *(calls)* Run away quick! The caretaker will hold you for the police.

Head *(quietly as if talking to the **Other Student**)* Yes, stay there . . . out of the way you silly thing. *(To the **Student**.)*

You've chosen a confrontation you can't win. The police will be here in a moment. Glaring doesn't hurt me. How weak you are! You can feel it. Of course you can. All bullies are weak.

Other Student (*off. Calls*)   Please leave him alone!

Head (*mutters*)   The silly little . . . (*Calls to the* **Other Student**.) Stay there! I forbid you to come any nearer!

Other Student (*off. Calls*)   Don't talk to him! He'll do something!

The **Student** *takes out a knife.*

Other Student (*off. Screams*)   No!

Head   Don't be stupid. Put it away. I shall never let you in now.

Other Student (*off. Calls*)   Don't! Don't! I told you!

Head (*to the* **Other Student**)   Be quiet! (*To the* **Student**.) If you go away now you can say you didn't come here to cause harm. You came to get your own back by frightening me with the knife. You were playing the big hero. You needn't run, you can walk away. I won't take away your dignity. If you –

Other Student (*off. Calls*)   Please! Please!

Head (*to the* **Other Student**)   Go to the corner! You encourage him! He's doing it for an audience! (*Slight pause. More gently.*) You don't know what you're involved in. You young people don't know what you're doing. I can't let you in with a knife. (*Sudden anger.*) If you must use it, use it on yourself! You haven't the guts! (*Calmer.*) I stand here for the children's sake. I don't want to. What does it matter to me what you do or where you go? Why did I have to meet you in this gate? How silly it all is.

The **Student** *stabs the* **Head**. *The* **Head** *staggers forwards.*

Other Student (*off. Calls*)   Don't! Don't!

The **Other Student** *runs in and catches hold of the* **Head**. *The*

Head *staggers, bent double.*

Head (*pushing the* **Other Student** *away*) Go – go – he'll hurt you –

The **Head** *staggers through the gateway into the school yard. The* **Other Student** *follows the* **Head***, backing away from the* **Student***.*

Other Student (*tears*) No no no.

The **Student** *stands alone with the knife. He walks a few steps towards the gate. Off, the sounds of the children's agitation.*

Other Student (*off*) Teacher's dead! Teacher can't move!

Off, the children shout in fear. The **Student** *goes to the gate and looks into the school yard. He stops. The children fall silent. He raises a foot – for a moment it is poised – then he brings it down inside the gate. A single cry from the children. He throws the knife into the yard. It clatters. Silence. He turns and runs down the street.*

Lesson

The **Weapons Instructor** *comes on in army denims and carrying a rifle.*

Instructor (*calls*) Red flag.

Off, an indistinct acknowledgement.

Instructor *slots the magazine into the rifle. The* **Student** *comes on in army denims.* **Instructor** *gives him the rifle.*

Instructor Firing in the prone position. Down.

Student *lies on the ground and aims the rifle towards the butts.*

Instructor All of human history is in the rifle. Savages who threw stones – used the first slings – shot the first arrows – helped to make the rifle. The first miners dug for ore – the first smelters made metal for pots and pans – and later it was refined to make the barrel. The first smiths

created the skills to shape it. Flint-knappers made the firing
pan that led to the modern firing mechanism. Ore and flint
were got through trade. So there had to be ships and roads
and markets and accountants. Alchemists tried to turn dirt
into gold. They taught chemists who discovered gunpowder.
Technologists invented the bore so the rifle shot further and
truer. They invented the optic for night sight that cured
our natural blindness in darkness. Inventions are made
when we're ready to use them. If armies that fought with
spears were suddenly given rifles they'd have exterminated
each other as if they had nuclear weapons. You wouldn't
be here. Nor would TV, planes, computers. All those things
are in that rifle. Sniper and assault weapon combined.
Weight four kilograms. Barrel thirty-three inches. Calibre
Standard NATO 7.6. Muzzle velocity 2900 feet a second –
860 metres a second. Gas operated. Image intensification
using wavelength of visible light. Infrared night sight. Your
hands are holding the history of science – the modern
world. Respect the rifle. Handle it as a surgeon does a
scalpel in the brain. If you knock it it goes out of true.
Ready – get comfortable. Relaxed. Tension jerks the gun:
you pull the shot. It doesn't kill. Safety catch. (**Student**
releases the safety catch and follows the rest of the instructions.)
Finger in the trigger guard. Aim at the base of the
cardboard soldier. Gently pull the trigger finger towards
you gathering the slack on the trigger. When you feel the
resistance you've reached the firing point. Hold it. Carefully
raise the sight up the cardboard soldier – carefully, gently –
to the concentric circles on the chest. As the sight rises into
the circles and moves to the centre – just as it touches it:
squeeze.

Student *fires a shot.*

Instructor   Safety catch.

Student *engages the safety catch.*

Voice (*off*)   Inner.

Instructor   Improvement. Next time a bull's-eye. Up.

Student *stands.* **Instructor** *reaches behind and takes the bayonet from its belt frog.* **Instructor** *clips the bayonet to the rifle.*

Instructor (*shouts*) Haa! What is it now? Knife! Blade! Chopper! The oldest thing in the world! Haa! Haa! Grab it – grip it – get it! Harder! Harder! Deadman's grip! Practice for when yer're dead! (*Demonstrates.*) Lunge! Thrust! Parry! Jab! Kill! In! Twist! Out! Haa! Haa! (*Holds out rifle to* **Student**.) Take it! (**Student** *takes rifle.*) Grab it – grip it – get it! Harder! Harder! Haa! Haa! Throttle it! Lunge! Thrust! Jab! Kill! Kill! Kill!

Student *gestures with the rifle.*

Instructor Kill it! Kill it! Give us! (*Snatches the rifle from* **Student**.) Grab it – grip it – get it! Harder! Stab it! Jab! Cut! Haa! Haa! In! Twist! Out! Stick from the front! Always front! Front in the gut! 'E turns 'n runs? – don't stick 'im in the kidneys! Chase 'im! Trip 'im! Kick 'im – boot 'im over! Stick 'is gut – in the front! Why? Why? Why? (**Student** *can't answer.*) In the gut it 'urts! Man can't move! – inconvenience of a bayonet in the gut. Can't stick yer back! 'E knows 'e's dead while 'e's alive! Jab 'im! In! Twist! Out! Haa! Take it! (*Shoves the rifle into* **Student**'s *hands.*) Grab it – grip it – get it! Harder! Harder! Jab! Jab! In! Twist! Out! Practise that! Do it!

Instructor *goes out.* **Student** *stands still.* **Instructor** *comes back kicking along the ground a sack stuffed with straw and plastic packing.*

Instructor I said practise! (*Quietly.*) All the dead killed by all the rifles – their bones are in that rifle. If yer shook it yer'd 'ave a rattle for a giant. (*Kicks sack away from him along the ground.*) Let's see yer kill that. (**Student** *goes towards the sack.*) Halt! (**Student** *stops.*) Scream! Ha! Ha!

Student Ha!

Instructor Ha!

Student Ha!

Instructor Ha! Ha! Ha!

Student   Ha! Ha! Ha!

Instructor   Scream! Scare the animals! Scare God if there is one! Why? Why? Why? (**Student** *can't answer.*) Scream as if the bayonet's in *your* gut! Then the bloke yer're runnin at knows 'ow cold steel feels! Scream the dead man's scream! 'E 'ears 'e's dead while 'e's still alive!

Student (*screams*)

Instructor   More! More! More! Curdle 'is blood so it don't run out – it dribbles out like gravel! Kill 'im!

Student *sticks the bayonet in the sack.*

Instructor   Dear-o-dear. Yer disappoint me. I 'ad a shufties in the CO's office. Fingered the files. Saw yourn. Was I chuffed! Criminal 'form'! Majesty's pleasure – a misnomer if she 'ad anythin t' do with you. File said knife-man! Used a blade when 'e was a kid! Dear God – 'ardly bigger 'n a nipper! 'E'll teach me 'ow t' do it! Yer couldn't stick a 'atpin in a quiverin jelly!

Student *bayonets the sack.*

Instructor   You refusin to obey 'n order? (*Takes rifle.*) I said kill the sack! Not take a nap on it! Do it! Curtain a' blood before the eyes! Stick 'im so 'ard 'is blood splashes on the clouds! Up there! – that one! It can be done! I'll sit 'ere 'n let it drizzle on my picnic! Let me see it get up 'n run when it sees yer comin! Kill it!

Instructor *screams and runs round in circles – then repeatedly bayonets the sack. Savage but efficient. Steps back and hands the rifle to* **Student**.

Instructor   Do likewise. A tip. A little refinement. Trick of the trade. When the bayonet penetrates the guts it's apt to become encumbered. To prevent this eventuality dislodge the carcass from yer bayonet with yer boot. (*Demonstrates.*) In. (*He lunges the bayonet into the sack.*) Twist. (*He twists the bayonet.*) Boot. (*He stamps his boot on the sack.*) Out. (*He withdraws the bayonet.*) Ha! (*Shoves the rifle at* **Student**.) Grab it – grip it – get it! Harder! Run!

Student *runs in circles.*

Instructor   Faster! Faster! 'E's 'n errand boy 'arf asleep on 'is mornin paper-round! Faster! Scream! Haa! Kill it!

Student *screams and lunges the bayonet into the sack. The sack is stuck on the bayonet – he spins round in despair – trying to shake off the sack – groans – nightmare – spinning round and round with the sack on the end of the bayonet.*

Instructor   Idiot! Idiot! Boot it off! Boot! Mind that bloody – ! Boot it!

Student *pulls the sack from the end of the bayonet. For a moment stuck with it in his arms – lurches – half-dance – falls – kicks it away.*

Instructor   Clown! Clown! Yer could 'a ripped me! In a war yer're dead! Dead! . . . (*Looks at watch.*) . . . Clean up this mess. Period's over. Litter on the parade ground. Clown.

Instructor *goes out.* **Student** *stands. Picks up the sack and scattered straw. Goes out.*

Reccy

A **Soldier** *comes on in battledress with rifle, IC (intercom) and bins (binoculars).*

Soldier (*to IC*)   Reccy to platoon. Tower due north three thousand metres. MR 347 291. Stone. Two floors. Big roof – loft maybe. Door. Two windows each floor. All this aspect. Skylight in roof – tiles gone maybe, sniper slit maybe. No enemy sighting over.

IC crackles and stops. **Student** *comes on in battledress with rifle and bins.*

Soldier   Anything there?

Student *crouches by* **Soldier**. *Bins the tower.*

Student   No – dead.

Soldier   And here.

Student   They was there yesterday.

Soldier   Done a runner.

Student   What is it anyway? Map say?

Soldier (*shrugs*)   Stone tower middle of nowhere.

Student   Hunting lodge.

Soldier   Reckon it's tunnelled so they can nip in 'n out out of sight?

Student   No cover to hide an entrance. Out there on its jack-tod.

IC crackles and stops.

Soldier (*to IC*)   Reccy receiving over. (*IC crackles and stops.*) Will do out. (*Repeating IC to* **Student**.) If there's any other structures?

Student   He's got a map.

Soldier   Means temporary in nature.

Student (*bins*)   Tell him no. Just grass.

Soldier (*to IC*)   Reccy reporting. No just a lot of grass over. (*IC crackles and stops.*) Will do and out. (*Repeating IC to* **Student**.) Having a chat.

Student (*bins*)   Quiet. Empty windows. Trees felled to open up the field of fire ... Why's the door shut if they scarpered?

Soldier   Trap?

IC crackles and stops.

Soldier (*to IC*)   Reccy receiving over. (*IC crackles and stops.*) Understood and out. (*To* **Student**.) Platoon's moving up. Rendezvous here one hour.

Student   Means two if they're in their usual rush. (*Lowers bins. Nods.*) Wait out of sight in the ditch.

Soldier   Brew up?

Student   Yeh down in the – hey up! . . . (*Bins.*) Get on that thing.

Soldier   What's – . . . ? (*To IC.*) Reccy to platoon.

Student (*bins. Slow*)   Hold on . . . something going on in – back from the window – see more than one of them – can't see into the room, not clear – they're chucking out a – from the window. They're hanging out a white sheet.

Soldier (*to IC*)   White sheet corp. (*To **Student**.*) That's that then.

Student (*bins. Puzzled*)   White something. But why – it's knotted –

Soldier (*to **Student***)   Come on. (*Refers to IC.*) He'll be going bonkers. (*To IC.*) Just reporting corp.

Student (*bins*)   Got it. They didn't have a white sheet. They knotted their vests together.

Soldier (*to **Student***)   That desperate! (*To IC.*) Oke' corp white sheet on tower over.

IC crackles.

Student (*bins*)   One two three –

Soldier   They coming out?

Student   Counting the vests. Tell us how many inside.

IC stops.

Soldier (*to IC*)   Still checking corp.

Student (*bins*)   Tell him to stay on alert when they come up. Could be enemy in the grass. Wind shaking it. Can't tell if enemy moving in it.

IC crackles and stops.

Soldier (*to **Student***)   He's getting on to Company HQ for orders.

Student Tell him we'll sit it out in the ditch.

Soldier (*to IC*) Reccy to platoon. We'll rendezvous in the ditch. Your map – same ref as previous. Advise stay on alert. Tall grass. Windy. Could give enemy cover over. (*IC crackles. To* **Student**.) They've put the major on. (*IC stops. To IC*.) Reccy reporting sir. Confirm white flag stone tower sir. MR 347 291 over. (*IC crackles briefly. Stops. To IC*.) Confirm stone tower sir. Company 'C' came under small arms fire from tower yesterday approx 17.30 hours over.

IC crackles.

Student What war's he fighting? Boer war?

IC stops.

Soldier (to **Student**) Says tell him how many.

Student (*bins. Counts*) I make that ... ten vests.

Soldier (*to IC*) Reccy reporting sir. Ten vests –

Student Men! Tell him men or he'll be confirming all night.

Soldier Ten men sir. Repeat ten men sir over.

IC crackles and stops.

Soldier (*to IC*) Reccy confirming understood sir. Will do and out. (*To* **Student**.) He says go forward and take the surrender.

Student Two of us?

Soldier Said the sheet might be bluff. Seen we're two. Worked out we're advance reccy. Hang sheet out to keep us sitting while they call up reinforcements. Trap platoon. Reckons if they fired on 'C' yesterday why're they jacking it in today?

Student Obvious – had enough. It's a general retreat everywhere. Stranded here in the grass? All they want's home.

Soldier Want to tell him?

Student   We do his dirty work. He rolls up in his armoured truck. Let's move.

Soldier *and* **Student** *release their safety catches and go towards the tower.*

Roof

An **Enemy Soldier** *comes in in battle dress and balaclava. Rifle slung on back. Carries blanket. Looks up and round.*

Enemy   Under the roof. Good builders. They could cut beams. Little window. Birds in and out. Droppings on the stone sill. They turned to stone. No one here for years.

Sits on ground.

Talking to myself. We're all half-mad now.

From the blanket he takes a toddler's toy train. It is made by a local carpenter. Wooden, squat, robust, painted in faded primary colours. Stares at it. Spins the wheel with a finger.

Why did they leave you here? Played in the tower while the big people killed the game? Why didn't you come back? Take it with you? Was it such a rush? Lost it in the corner? (*Shakes the train.*) Spiders.

Places the train on the floor. Looks at it.

We should've buried him. My mate yesterday. Shot. Carried him outside. We didn't wait. Maybe snipers in the grass. Can't tell. The wind. Foxes – rats – 'll eat him. Take bits to their young.

Pushes the train along the ground.

Voice (*off. Calls*)   Hey!

Enemy *listens in silence for a moment.*

Enemy   He wrote my letters home. Told him things I never told before. For the letters. He read what my wife said to me . . . When the kitchen door's open you see people in the street. Little metal noises the saucepans and kettle make. (*Drapes himself in the blanket.*) Sunny yesterday. Saw their backs bobbing in the grass. Captain opened fire. It's always them or us. Shot him in the face. When it's over –

Voice (*off*)   Hey – you up there?

Enemy   – they'll collect them all together. Bury them in one place. They think I've run. (*Pushes the train along the ground.*) We should've buried him. Choo – . . . Sleep. (*Kicks the train away.*) The captain's run. Said he was going out to reccy. He won't come back. They don't answer the radio any more. (*Looks up at roof.*) I could sleep up there. Sleep in the quiet. Must keep my head fit.

Stands draped in the blanket. Goes out.

Tower

A hanging: ten army issue vests knotted into a sheet.

Student *and* **Soldier** *come on with rifles at the ready.*

Soldier (*to IC*)   Reccy at tower proceeding over.

IC brief crackle. Stops.

Student   Take the door. Keep to the wall. I'll call them out. Send them down the track. Hold them in the dip.

Soldier   Oke'.

Soldier *goes out.*

Student (*shouts to tower*)   Out! Out! Out!

Slight pause.

Soldier (*off*) Hands up! Hands up! That way! Path!

Student (*shouts*)   One at a time! One – one – one! Out!

Soldier (*off*)   Down! Path! Path! After him! Move it! I'm pointing – path!

Student   Keep coming! Keep coming!

Prisoner (*off*)   Mabsvd acsbvacxs vczxdafs dafs czx czsda –

Student (*shouts*)   Shut it! No chat! Only dead chummies chat here! Move!

Soldier (*off*)   Shut it! Shut it! That path! Down there! Keep on that!

Student *watches the prisoners going down the path to the dip.*

Student   Right . . . (*Sudden shout of command.*) Sit! Down! Sit! (*Half imitates squatting.*) Down! Down! Sit!

Soldier (*off*)   Hands on head! Hands on head! Like this! Watch me! Savvy? Yeah – keep 'em there! (*Slight pause. Calls.*) That the lot?

Student   You got ten.

Soldier (*off. Sudden order*)   Stay sat!

Student   I'll check the windows.

Student *goes out in the direction opposite to the* **Prisoners**.

Soldier *comes in, still watching the* **Prisoners**.

Soldier (*calls to* **Student**)   That lot won't be trouble.

Student *comes in.*

Student   Empty. You got a full house.

Soldier   Watch from here. The platoon'll bring trucks.

Student (*going*)   Check inside for loot.

Student *goes out in the direction of the* **Prisoners**.

Soldier (*to IC*)   Reccy to platoon. Ten POW bagged. No exchange of fire over.

IC crackles. **Soldier** *laughs. IC stops.*

Soldier (*to IC*)   Reccy to platoon. Yeh funny very good never thought of that –

Student *comes in.*

Soldier (*to IC*)   Hold on – (**Student** *shakes head. To IC.*) Checked out inside clear over.

IC crackles.

Student   Had a quick run up and down. Rifles not even stacked. Dropped all over the floor. Eaten all their grub. Mess.

IC stops.

Student (*squats*)   My sort of war: their hands on their heads. Pathetic sods all in.

Soldier   Suppose I ought to interrogate?

Student (*shakes head*)   Let the IO earn his dinner. Watch 'em from here. Good view all round. Stay into the wall. Could be more in the grass.

Soldier   Everything's a risk here.

Student *and* **Soldier** *sit by the wall with a hand on their rifles.*

Student   Can't go on long. They'll lose interest. It was over a month ago. Few weeks – home.

Soldier   Saw a body out the back.

Student   One of theirs.

Soldier   Yeah. Brew up?

Student   No I'll do a prowl round in a minute. Brew after.

Soldier   Don't reckon the next few weeks.

Student   O?

Soldier   We're tempting –

Student (*sudden shout. Stands*)   Oi! Up! Up! On head! You understand! – up! (*Gestures with rifle.*) Keep 'em up! Any more of you and I'll be down with this! (*Sits. Shouts.*) Scratch when the war's over! That's the time to celebrate!

Soldier   – tempting our luck. Each day I wait till it's dark
and say one less to go. They give themselves up. Yesterday
they tried to kill us. Tomorrow their mates'll be at it.
Someone's luck runs out. Someone has to be the last one
killed in every war.

Student   Least they chose a good pad. Out the weather.
Look at 'em. Kids. Chuffed it's over. Their officers dropped
'em 'ere an' scarpered. But if they came back those kids'd
get fell in as if –

Shot. **Soldier** *falls. Dead.* **Student** *dives to the side, slithering
over the ground – rolls over – backs up to wall. He doesn't know
where the shot came from.*

Prisoners (*off. Calling*)   Mansvb! Mansvb! Caxzas!
Mavqsdfags –

Student *goes out.*

Prisoners (*off. Calling*)   Mansb! Navazxc dfdsa wdweasq!
Sdfg!

Enemy *comes from tower carrying a rifle.*

Prisoners (*off. Calling*)   Nabcsdf! Mavsdfdafsd saxdf sdgf
aswd!

Enemy (*lowers rifle*)   Mansbv . . . (*Distressed. Calls to*
Prisoners.) Mavsac dgfsdc adserw xac axzs casfdge –

Student *comes on aiming his rifle at* **Enemy**.

Student   Up! Up! Hands up!

Prisoners (*off. Calling*)   Bavdasc ghfes –

Student (*shouting back at* **Prisoners**)   Shut it!

Enemy (*putting hands up*)   Manxvcafds cavscxdas! Vagfdas
mdsvs . . .

Covering **Enemy** *with his rifle,* **Student** *goes to* **Enemy**'s *rifle
and takes it aside. Goes to* **Soldier** *and checks the body. The IC
crackles and from time to time is silent, waiting for a response to its
calls.*

Student   Bastard. You bastard.

Student *starts to drag out the* **Soldier**'s *body, still covering*
Enemy. *The IC starts to crackle.* **Student** *drags the body off.*

Enemy (*calling to* **Prisoners**)   Nabcsxas! Mardsf caxdgws
chadfs –

Prisoners (*off. Calling to* **Enemy**)   Manxvc! Manxvc!
Mancs bxv das!

Enemy *backs a few paces.* **Student** *comes on. He covers*
Enemy *with his rifle. The IC dangles from his other hand. It still*
crackles from time to time.

Student (*to* **Enemy**)   How many? (*Gestures to tower.*) Savvy?
Show me! Fingers! How many?

Enemy (*uncomprehending*)   Manvsb . . . Navzcxb czxsa . . .

Student   None? That none? You last?

Enemy   . . . Vacxads . . .

Student (*to IC*)   Reccy to platoon. (*IC crackles briefly and*
stops.) Sorry sir yes sir over. (*IC crackles briefly and stops.*) Sorry
sir. Carter sir. Dead. Sniper. Tower. Over. (*IC crackles.*
Mutters to himself.) Sod it – it'll be my soddin fault . . . (*IC*
stops. To IC.) Sir confirming Carter dead sir. Sniper in
tower over. (*IC crackles. Mutters to himself.*) Rabbit rabbit on
and on . . . (*IC stops. To IC.*) No sir – clear now. Platoon
can move up. I killed the sniper. Over.

Enemy (*weakly pleading while* **Student** *talked to the*
IC)   Mabvsc bavcxads . . . vzcxbcv . . . vzcda cad srewcad
qweas . . .

IC crackles briefly and stops.

Student (*to* **Enemy**)   None minus one is you chummy.
(*Gestures with rifle.*)

Enemy (*calls in panic to* **Prisoners**)   Bacvsd! Manbscda!
Gfsdv xazds! Dacs gfsdvcad aweq czxsds xaz –

Student (*taking bayonet from belt frog*)   Too late sonny. Your mates can't help you! That's much too late!

Enemy (*terror. To* **Student**)   Mansbvx! Bavxzcsd!

Student (*shows bayonet to* **Enemy**. *Explains*)   This. Kill you.
See. Don't waste bullet. Keep them to help my mates. Do
this before the major's here. He'd tuck you in bed and kiss
you. Geneva Conventions type.

Enemy (*calls to* **Prisoners**)   Naabxvcz! Nabxvxz! (*Gestures
frantically to bayonet.*) Hrsdga! Zvslt! Gsdags –

A **Prisoner** *comes on. He is dressed identically to* **Enemy**, *with
a balaclava.*

Student   Out!

Enemy (*to* **Prisoner**)   Nabxvs fads cwedasqv fadsfs –
(*Points to roof of tower.*) – mbaczad xaesdwq wasd – cav
decfs –

Prisoner (*to* **Student**)   He shot – he didn't knowed –
he –

Student   Out! Back! I'll blast you back!

Prisoner   No – you mistooks sir – he didn't knowed sir –
the mans had –

IC starts to crackle. **Student** *swings his rifle to aim at* **Prisoner**.

Student   Out!

Prisoner *turns and starts to run out.*

Enemy (*screaming after* **Prisoner**)   Mansxv! Bavaczx fads!
Faxsd xvas afsadwgers nacds fads –

Prisoner *turns and starts to run back to* **Student**.

Prisoner   Sir –

Student   Back! Nothing to do with you!

Enemy (*pleading with* **Prisoner**)   Davcxz adasfd cadsw
axsdfwg adzxsv! Facswgeda! Daxzd! Daxzd! Gavscad!
Sdaxz –

Student   What is it? What's he say?

Prisoner   Say he didn't knowed – not knowing – of nothing – we give surrender he did not knowed –

Student *switches off the IC.*

Student (*to* **Enemy**)   Yeah! – surrendered! (*To* **Prisoner**.) Tell him!

Prisoners (*off. Calling*)   Maxzvba vacdsfa sgds! Navzc dsrfee daxs –

Prisoner (*shouting to* **Prisoners**)   Manvcs! Acds! (*The* **Prisoners** *are silent. To* **Enemy**.) Man bzvxcz da fsdaqw bavds – (*Pointing to the hanging vests.*) – nabvxcd fsda –

Enemy (*to* **Prisoner**)   Brxds? (*Turns to look at the vests.*) . . . Mvacds brads navzcs resdfa –

Student   What's he say?

Prisoner   Say he didn't knowed we give white sign to show –

Student   Didn't know? He was with you! In there!

Prisoner (*to* **Enemy**)   Bacxzd gfdsa? Fdacsxwg rets?

Enemy (*to* **Prisoner**)   Bacxzd gfsda! – navdsa fgdwg xvss –

Prisoner (*to* **Enemy**)   Dacdsqqw –

Enemy (*to* **Prisoner**)   Bracdsa –

Prisoner (*to* **Enemy**)   Dsfga! (*To* **Student**.) He says he was sleeps. In top. (*Points to roof of tower.*) Sleeps – in you say – how is that? – navczx – mvanavczx – in *attics*!

Student   Sleeps? With a war outside? I believe that!

Student *is fiddling with bayonet. He is too agitated to fix it.*

Enemy   Nvacxads daxsfda cvzx mnches vads –

Prisoner   He say wear vest. Say tell man vest. Is wearing – see? Didn't knowed. (*To* **Enemy**.) Cavxcxz mnches bacvs.

Enemy (*to* **Prisoner**)   Mnches bavcasdfg!

Student   He must've knowed!

Enemy *is taking off his jacket.*

Prisoner   Is proof! Is proof! Is wearing vest!

Student   Who let him sleep? When he's dead let him blame you!

Enemy's *jacket is off.*

Enemy (*pointing at vest, plucking it*)   Mnches! Mnches! Vaca das czvx dxzfsx adsfg –

Student (*fiddling with bayonet*)   When he looked out the window – saw you sat – hands on heads – he knows!

Prisoner   He say sleep still in eye – he didn't knowed – he good man – vest proof –

Student   He saw my mate! – wake enough to shoot!

Prisoner   Please sir – please my friend –

Enemy *takes off the vest.*

Student   You set us up! Turn our backs! *He* shoots!

Enemy (*holding out the vest, offering it to* **Student**)   Mnches ... mnches ... abczvxda ... vczxq bzcvxc daxs ... mnches ... (*Reaches the vest out further.*) mnches ... vzcxa vxzcds –

Student (*fiddling with bayonet*)   Damn it! In! Get in! Come on!

Prisoner (*pointing at bayonet*)   Yes yes you kill is soldier. Not that my friend. If you kill not that. Please not good. Not that. So is not right. For no ones.

Enemy *is on his knees holding the vest to his face and crying into it.*

Enemy   Nabcxvxas. Nabczxsd. Hgweads. Dfasczxs.

Student (*bayonet fixed*)   All of you! – in it! You want him shot? I start shooting I won't stop! Shoot the lot! A little heap of bodies – nice!

Prisoner   Is not right. (*Tries to go to* **Enemy**.) Nabxc
xzcdasa dfs –

Student (*to* **Prisoner**)   Up! Up!

Prisoner *stops. Puts hands up.* **Enemy** *is on his knees. He has
stopped crying and holds out the vest in silence.*

Student (*pointing off to the dead* **Soldier**)   My mate dead!
See that? You in half a second! Slept! You'll take the
longest sleep!

Enemy *holds out the vest. Eyes shut.* **Student** *bayonets him. He
boots the body off the bayonet.*

Student   Ha!

Prisoners (*off*)   Barcaxzsd! Bavzcsd! Vzcxadsf vxaczds
fads!

Silence. **Prisoner** *stands with his hands up.* **Enemy** *is sprawled.*
Student *steps away, picks up* **Enemy**'*s vest and wipes his
bayonet clean on it. Drops the vest. Switches on the IC – instantly it
crackles.* **Student** *waits in silence for it to stop.*

Student (*to IC*)   Reccy reporting 'A' Platoon. Temporary
bother sir. Sorry. Chummy on roof. Hiding. Berserker. No
time to reload. Stuck him. Over.

IC crackles. **Student** *looks up and sees* **Prisoner** *still standing
with hands up.*

Student (*to* **Prisoner**)   Down there. Get. With your
mates. Your lucky day.

Prisoner *goes. IC stops crackling.*

Student (*to IC*)   Carter won't need a medic sir.
Confirming dead. Over. (*IC crackles and stops.*) Yes sir keep
an eye on POWs till platoon –

Student *stops. He sees that* **Enemy** *has sat up.*

Enemy   . . . nbzvcx . . . bcaxzs . . . shte shte shte . . .

Enemy *picks up the vest and starts to clean the bayonet on it.*

Student   Don't do that.

Enemy *(cleaning)*   ... shte ... shte. ...

Student *goes to* **Enemy**. *Takes the vest. Throws it away.*

Student   Don't do that.

Starts to walk away.

Enemy *(speaking into space)*   Bvacan bvagchteus.

Student *stops. Turns to* **Enemy**.

Enemy *(repeats)*   Bvacan bvagchteus.

Student *(coming back)*   Don't do that.

Enemy *(repeats)*   Bvacan bvag –

Student *bayonets* **Enemy**. *Dead.*

Student *(calls)*   Haa! Haa! Take it! Take it! Double!

Prisoner *runs in.*

Student   Take it! Your mates! ... haa ...

Prisoner *starts to take out* **Enemy**'s *body.*

Student   Hvacan brasdghes.

Prisoner *stops. Turns to look at* **Student**.

Student   What does it mean?

Prisoner *stares blankly at* **Student**, *the body slumped at his feet.*

Student   Hvacan brascgaese.

Prisoner   Nothing sir.

Student   It must mean – some – ! What's it say?

Prisoner *stares.*

Student   Tell your mates to bury him.

Prisoner *starts to take out the body again.*

Student   You heard him when he – . . . ?

Prisoner *goes on taking out the body.*

Student   It means *something*!

Prisoner *stops and stares.*

Student   Hshdaca brazxcgzca? Brs – brs – chavsa – what would – do your people say when – ?

Student *sits down against the wall.* **Prisoner** *turns and starts to take out the body.*

Student   Fadxz fadxscvzx? Hadfs czxa dfgsfd? . . . Bvache . . .

Prisoner (*stops*)   Is nothing sir . . . Is buffalo . . . table . . .

Student   Hdvas – fasdfgd – hvasd.

Prisoner   Water. Buffalo.

Student *stares at* **Prisoner**.

Student   Take it.

Prisoner *takes out the body.* **Student** *stands, picks up the two rifles and the vest. Looks at the* **Prisoners**.

Student (*calls*)   Chvas – ? Cha – ?

Silence. **Student** *goes to the hanging vests and tugs them down. Takes them out with him.*

Four Documents

Document One

Philip Lawrence was a 'good' headmaster. Government,
church, press praised him for getting to grips with a 'bad'
school . . . He expelled sixty of his pupils. They were put
onto the street. And then one day he stood in his school
gateway and violence returned. He was killed. That
meeting in the gateway might have been imagined by
Dostoevsky in a novel or Sophocles in a play. Perhaps he
was killed by one of the pupils he'd expelled. But that
would have been only a detail. I'm sure Philip Lawrence
was as innocent as his killer. But in one shape or another,
violence always returns to unleash its wrath on the
ignorance that creates it. And we are an ignorant society.

At the Inland Sea (p. 80) by Edward Bond – in the 'Notes
and Commentary' (published by Methuen)

Document Two

September 20
We finally got through by jeep to Salerno, but found a
battle still going on in the outskirts of the town. German
mortar bombs were exploding in the middle of a small
square only a hundred yards from Security Headquarters.
Here I saw an ugly sight: a British officer interrogating an
Italian civilian, and repeatedly hitting him about the head
with a chair; treatment which the Italian, his face a mask
of blood, suffered with stoicism. At the end of the
interrogation, which had not been considered successful, the
officer called in a private of the Hampshires and asked him
in a pleasant, conversational sort of manner, 'Would you
like to take this man away, and shoot him?' The private's
reply was to spit on his hands, and say, 'I don't mind if I
do, sir.' The most revolting episode I have seen since

joining the forces.

Naples '44 (p. 21) by Norman Lewis

Document Three

... a wide circle of troops of his brigade surrounding a two-storied pillbox, and firing at a loophole in the upper story from which shots were coming. One man, coolly standing close below and firing up at it, fell back killed but the Germans in the lower chamber soon after surrendered. The circle of Australians at once assumed easy attitudes, and the prisoners were coming out when shots were fired, killing an Australian. The shot came from the upper storey, whose inmates knew nothing of the surrender of the men below; but the surrounding troops were much too heated to realise this. To them the deed appeared to be the vilest treachery, and they forthwith bayoneted the prisoners. One [Australian], about to bayonet a German, found that his own bayonet was not on his rifle. While the wretched man implored him for mercy, he grimly fixed it and then bayoneted the man.

'The Face of Battle' (p. 48–9) by John Keegan, from *The Australian Official History of the Great War*

Document Four

22 After these things God tested Abraham, and said to him, 'Abraham!' And he said, 'Here am I.' [2]He said, 'Take your son, your only son Isaac, whom you love, and go to the land of Mori'ah, and offer him there as a burnt offering upon one of the mountains of which I shall tell you.' [3]So Abraham rose early in the morning, saddled his ass, and took two of his young men with him, and his son Isaac; and he cut the wood for the burnt offering, and arose and went to the place of which God had told him. [4]On the third day Abraham lifted up his eyes and saw the

place afar off. [5]Then Abraham said to his young men, 'Stay here with the ass; I and the lad will go yonder and worship, and come again to you.' [6]And Abraham took the wood of the burnt offering, and laid it on Isaac his son; and he took in his hand the fire and the knife. So they went both of them together. [7]And Isaac said to his father Abraham, 'My father!' And he said, 'Here am I, my son.' He said, 'Behold, the fire and the wood; but where is the lamb for a burnt offering?' [8]Abraham said, 'God will provide himself the lamb for a burnt offering, my son.' So they went both of them together.

[9]When they came to the place of which God had told him, Abraham built an altar there, and laid the wood in order, and bound Isaac his son, and laid him on the altar, upon the wood. [10]Then Abraham put forth his hand, and took the knife to slay his son. [11]But the angel of the LORD called to him from heaven, and said, 'Abraham, Abraham!' And he said, 'Here am I.' [12]He said, 'Do not lay your hand on the lad or do anything to him; for now I know that you fear God, seeing you have not withheld your son, your only son, from me.' [13]And Abraham lifted up his eyes and looked, and behold, behind him was a ram, caught in a thicket by his horns; and Abraham went and took the ram, and offered it up as a burnt offering instead of his son.

The Book of Genesis

Tuesday

Tuesday was first broadcast by BBC TV Education in March 1993, with the following cast:

Father	Bob Peck
Brian	Ben Chaplin
Irene	Natalie Morse
First PC	Che Walker
Second PC	Matthew Lloyd Lewis
Third PC	Niall Refoy
Senior Officer	Richard Cubison
Neighbour	Tracie Hart
Medic	Colin Bourner
Child	Elliot Henderson-Boyle
WPC	Suzy Cooper

Produced by Richard Langridge
Directed by Edward Bond *and* Sharon Miller

Note

Tuesday was commissioned by BBC TV Education and first broadcast in three weekly parts. These parts are shown on this script. But as the play occurs in 'real time' – the time is continuous – it need not be divided into separate parts.

The play has been staged in this version. No interval is necessary but there could be one at or a little before the ending of Part Two.

When the play was filmed the police and medics were used in an elaborate way. They could be staged more simply. It depends on the nature of the production – for example on the number of players and amount of equipment available.

Characters

Father
Brian
Irene
First PC
Second PC
Third PC
Fourth PC
Senior Officer
First Medic
Neighbour
Child
WPC

Policemen, Medics

Setting

A small upstairs bedroom in a suburban pre-war house converted to flats. A window. Outside it the roofs of the houses and factories in a light industrial suburb. When the brick-red window curtains are drawn light filters through the material. On the wall, two posters or unframed prints and a framed picture of Colley Wood, showing the sea seen through trees. A free-standing wardrobe – a dress hangs on the outside on a clothes-hanger. A neatly made single bed with a middling-to-dark blue coverlet. Slippers by the bed. Below the window a chair and table used as a dressing-table and a desk. On the table some test exam papers, a few reference books, a plastic ruler, a green eraser and a ceramic pot holding five or six biros and pencils.

for Richard Langridge

Part One

*Irene sits in a chair at the desk. She is in her mid-teens. She wears a skirt, blouse and an open cardigan. She is answering questions in a set of test exam papers. She is lost in thought as she considers which question to answer next. Then she begins to write, looking slightly sideways at the ball of the biro. Silence except for **Irene**'s hand on the paper. A doorbell rings downstairs. **Irene** ignores it and goes on writing. The doorbell rings again. After a moment's pause she makes a small sound of annoyance and goes on writing. Pause.*

Irene (*calls*) Dad.

*A moment's silence and then the doorbell again – a long persistent ring. Without changing her expression or making a sound **Irene** stops writing, puts down her biro and goes out. She leaves the door open.*

Silence. The sound of four feet running upstairs.

(*Off.*) Who said you could go up!

Brian *comes in, followed by **Irene**. He is in his late teens. He has short hair and wears dark jeans and a dark windcheater over a shirt.*

Irene You've got leave! Why didn't you phone! (*She puts her arms round him.*) You want to surprise me!

Brian *leaves **Irene** and shuts the door.*

Irene Dad'll be back.

Brian *goes to the bed and sits on the side.*

Irene What is it? Something's the matter.

Brian *looks at her a moment.*

Brian Done a runner.

Irene Oh. (*Slight pause.*) You've run away?

Brian Yes.

Irene   Why? Have you done something to . . . ?

Brian (*violently*)   No no! (*Immediately.*) *I've* done something! What chance – ! How can you make anyone understand? *I* haven't done it! It's not me!

Irene *stares at him.*

Brian (*calmer*)   I ran. That's all.

Irene   Why?

Brian   You've got to hide me.

Irene   Hide you? (*Bewildered.*) What've you done? This is stupid –

Brian   I told you I –

Irene (*suddenly trying to take control*)   What's happened? Did they do something to you? What? (*Sudden idea.*) Are they following you?

Brian   You've got to hide me. There's nowhere else now.

Irene   But they'll come here. Dad'll be back – any minute . . . (*Tries to think.*) Do your people know you're – ?

Brian   No no. I didn't go there. They wouldn't hide me.

Irene   The army'll go there. They'll give them our name. The army'll go everywhere you're known. They could be –

Brian   No – they don't know I've run. This morning – I walked out the barracks. I won't be missed yet.

Irene   Then you can go back – if you've done nothing to –

Brian   No.

Irene   Why not? (*Idea.*) Was there a fight?

Brian   Nothing, nothing happened. Let me stay. Tell the police you haven't seen me.

Irene (*trying to understand*)   You've run away. Are you hurt?

Brian *turns and lies face down on the bed.*

Brian No. Tired.

Irene (*stares at him*) If they've done something to you –
you mustn't run away – you'll put yourself in the wrong.

Brian (*face down on the bed*) I ask for help – isn't that
enough? . . . Help me.

Irene I am helping. Why've you run away? (*No answer.*)
Let me phone the barracks – the welfare. I'll tell them
you're ill. It's not helping you if I let you get into – I'll tell
them *I'm* ill. You stayed to help me to . . .

Brian (*face down*) I'm not going back.

Irene They'll come and take you back.

Brian (*low*) They may. They can. (*Into the blankets.*) But I
won't go. I won't *turn* in that direction. Never. (*Small and
intense.*) They'll have to turn the world round so the
barrack's facing me . . . I could lie here. Be asleep. Dream
it out. Make sense.

Irene You can't stay even if I said you could. You can't
just vanish! Dad's coming. The neighbours would see you
at the windows. They know you. If you're running away
you have to go further than this. God knows where! (*No
answer.*) This is silly.

Brian Then I can stay for a while? That's what you
meant, I heard you. Let me stay. I can think here.

Irene You can't think! If you could you'd tell me what
happened. The police'll tell me their version – not yours.

Brian It doesn't matter. They couldn't understand if I
told them. If they'd been there they wouldn't even have
seen it.

Irene *draws the curtains.*

Irene I'll have to manage. I'll try.

Brian *turns to face her.*

Brian I knew you'd let me.

Irene (*pause*)   D'you want a drink?

Brian   Not yet. (*Silence.*) The army doesn't know. No one does. Perhaps no one ever will. Or I'll wait for years and tell a stranger. No – it'd be too late. It's too late now. If I told anyone – and they couldn't understand – jeered – I wouldn't want to live. Not even with you.

Irene   I won't jeer.

Brian   No no, you wouldn't. That's strange. Being understood would be even worse than not being understood – in this world.

Irene (*not understanding*)   Worse? (*Frightened.*) Is it me? What have I done? (*Tries to think.*) Did I hurt anyone by – was it my letters? Tell me! – why are you here?

Brian   When I ran away this morning, I meant to go absent for a few days. Get drunk – spew it out of me – then go back like a corpse with a hangover. They'd welcome me with open arms – one of the lads had proved he rated! Now I can't. It's you. If I told you, you wouldn't let me go back. I know. (*Touches the bed at his side.*) Trust me.

Irene (*doesn't move*)   What am I being blamed for?

Brian   It's not blame. I don't know what it is. It must be thanks. I can't tell you – I can't hurt you. Because you're kind. (*Suddenly his mind drifts.*) Orders, orders. The army's always giving orders. They'd give orders to the hairs on a toothbrush.

Irene *turns to the door, unsure.*

Irene   Was that a key?

Brian *stands. Listens. Tense. Pause. He shakes his head.*

Irene   He went to the job centre. He should be back.

Brian (*flat*)   Perhaps he got an interview. (*He sits at the table.*) You were studying. Go on – don't let me hold you up.

Irene   Go on? You come here – do this – and tell me to
go on as if –

Brian   Why not? It's just thinking and writing it on
paper. (*Silence.*) A fly knows more about death than we do.
When you could die any second, you don't pray. You loot
instead. So you've got something to take home. You rob
the dead to show your guts still want you to live. God
doesn't help you, the dead do. Pehaps they pity you
because you're alive. I got an officer's pistol. Inlaid.

Irene (*quietly*)   The fighting's over. They can't send you
back now you're home. You're not running from that.

Brian   I'm not running. It's more serious: I walked . . . I
left so quietly my shadow's still back there looking for me.

Downstairs the sound of a door opening and closing.

Father (*off*)   Home!

Brian   Don't tell him. I'll hide – (*Bed.*) under there! I
won't be any – ! He doesn't come in here to –

Irene   Hide?

Brian   I'll be quiet. Really. I'm trained.

Father (*off*)   Is the kettle on?

Brian *tries to hide under the bed – it is too low.*

Irene *stares at him in astonishment.*

Irene   You can't hide! In this flat? You'd have to stop
breathing! Be invisible!

Brian   I don't want him here! I don't want his questions!
It's your room! You promised! He won't know – he doesn't
come in here!

Irene   He's my father. It's his house.

Irene *goes out and leaves the door open.* **Brian** *goes to it, pulls it
almost shut, listens at the crack. Then he shuts it and goes to the bed.
He unzips his windcheater and takes out an officer's elegant, inlaid
pistol. He hides it under the pillows. He sits at the desk. Stands. Sits*

on the bed.

A quiet tap on the door.

Slight pause before it opens. **Father** *pops his head and shoulders in. He is a bit thin but muscular. His face is bony, his eyebrows are a shade too thick, his hair is stubby. He wears slacks and a thickish jumper. He often jokes but has absolutely no sense of humour.*

Father All right if I . . . ? (*He comes in and shuts the door behind him. He speaks calmly and gently.*) Son what a surprise. Hello hello. Good to see you. Always. I told you to treat this place like home. Let's see you. (*He opens the curtains.*) That's better. Help yourself to the daylight: it's freebies. (*Turns to* **Brian**.) Oh it's you! I thought it was her other one! – Now what's all this about? Rene's got hold of some cock-'n'-bull story. You want to tell me? Take your time. Thank God you had the sense to come here and not somewhere else. We'll soon sort it out between us. Two heads eh? (*Pause.*) Job centre. You've got problems? Aaahhh. I don't know. Leak with a hole in it. The pits – wouldn't bury a dog in it if it'd bit me leg off. Come on lad – you're not getting yourself in trouble while I'm here. I'm too fond of you for that.

Brian I told her not to tell you.

Father (*mock surprise*) Not tell Dad? She's supposed to hide you under the bed? You have to get her to sweep it first! We're not thinking straight are we? If you're in trouble that's no reason to drag her in.

Irene *opens the door and stands in the doorway.*

Father Irene wait downstairs.

Irene I wanted to see if he's –

Father Wait down like a good girl. I'll handle this. I'll bring him down in a couple of shakes.

Irene *goes.*

Father (*shouts down through the open door*) I brought some shopping in. There's some stuff to go in the freezer. I couldn't get your yoghurt – I found something else. (*He shuts the door and turns to* **Brian**.) I can see you're upset. You don't have to tell me the ins and outs. I'll need to know – I'm curious anyway – but that can wait. The main thing's to catch it before it goes out of our hands. Rene says you went over the wall this morning? Right? So there's no great harm done so far. You went on a bender – young lad letting off steam – celebrate coming home in one piece – soon as you came round you reported back to the guardhouse. They'll understand – you'll be surprised. You'll lose a few weeks' wages. Finished. The family opposite've got a car. I'll borrow that and run you back. I'll pay for the petrol.

Brian   I have to talk to Irene.

Father   Yes Dad thank you very much. Why? You mean, to say goodbye?

Brian   You interrupted us – I hadn't finished.

Father   Oh dear I am sorry. Look lad I'm being patient with you. I don't think you appreciate your situation. You're not talking to Rene – even in my presence. I wouldn't even countenance it. You're not involving a girl her age. What sort of a father would I be if I encouraged you to do that? If I can't help you, I can look after her.

Brian   Five minutes. That's all I need to –

Father   No. You can tell me anything you've got to say. I'll pass it on if I consider it's appropriate. You're not hiding behind her. You've already managed to upset her once. That's why she defied me just now in the doorway. How d'you expect her to get ready for her exams in that state? If she messes them up her whole future's put in jeopardy. She'll know who to blame then. Now you show a bit of responsibility.

Brian   I'll go.

Father   No you won't. I'm not letting you run away from this – you're starting to make a habit of it. I want to know

what's going on. In this country we don't walk in and out
of people's houses just as we please. I'm not just her father.
I'm a member of the public. It's my responsibility to know
who we're letting loose on our streets. You tell me what
you're playing at.

Brian *goes to the door, opens it and calls down.*

Brian   Rene!

Calmly **Father** *reaches past* **Brian**, *pulls the door to till only a
crack is open and shouts through it.*

Father   Stay down there! I'm not playing about! I don't
want you up here – it's bad enough with him! (*He closes the
door and turns to* **Brian**.) Look lad. We'll start again. I'm
trying to be your friend but you're not making it easy. I
can't help you if you won't tell me what you've done.

Brian   I'm sorry I got you into this. I'll –

Father   Don't be sorry! I don't mind, it's my job! Haven't
you got that in your nut yet? Look. The fighting upset you
– them killing your mates – you killing them back. I know
all about it. I was in the army. It's worse for someone like
you. You're a considerate lad – good heart – that's why
Rene took you up. (*No response.*) Worse than that is it?
Something happened when you were out there – and you
chickened out: now the lads are ganging up on you? Well –
fine. You ran in the heat of the moment. Nothing to be
ashamed of – better men than you have done it. But if you
run now – when you're with friends trying to help – then
you've got a hard life ahead of you. (*Pause.*) I see. It's as
bad as that is it? – the officers. If you're being victimised
I'll be the first to stand up for you. You go back and hand
yourself in – if you don't play by the rules you get nowhere
– but there are crowds of people out there waiting to rally
round and help. We'll fight your corner. It's a free country
– wasn't that why you were fighting? We can take it to our
MP if we have to! (*No response.*) Your behaviour's telling me
you don't trust me lad. I'm sorry.

Brian *tries to go to the door.* **Father** *blocks his way.*

Brian (*flat*)   Please. Let me go.

Father (*low*)   Are you threatening me son?

Brian   Let me go.

Father   I don't know, there's some funny people about. He comes to my house. Invites himself upstairs. Upsets my daughter. Threatens me. Then when he doesn't get it all his own way he thinks he can walk off without so much as a by your leave. This is your prison. That door's shut till I say sesame (it happens to speak my language). Right, we've had our bit of fun. Now I'm telling you, not asking. I want to know what your game is. You could've murdered someone – put some old woman in hospital. You did *some* thing to get yourself in this state! The way you're carrying on isn't much of an assurance. If I let you through that door that makes me an accomplice of God knows –

Brian   No one knows I was here.

Father   My daughter knows. Am I supposed to lie in front of her? – your idea of a father-daughter relationship? Lad the more you say the less I like to hear. You always were a step out of line. She can't say I didn't warn her. Now, shall I call the police? They won't be so patient.

Brian *goes to the bed and sits on the side.*

Brian   I can't tell you.

Father   Oh? Why?

Brian   You wouldn't understand.

Father   Oh – I'm stupid? I don't believe I'm hearing this! You can tell my daughter – she's not stupid? It's Sonny Jim against the rest of the world!

Brian   I can't. I'm sorry. I don't know how. I can't make you understand. I wish I could!

Father *sits on the bed beside* **Brian**.

Father   You youngsters. All this fuss! In the end it's all nothing. The states Irene gets into – God knows why! I

wish you'd trust me. I could have it all wrapped up by
now. Finished and done with . . . I'm sorry I shouted. You
don't need that. Sometimes it all gets on top. You'll know,
when it's your turn. No work. The house needs attention.
I'd like to afford Irene a few extras – some fun with her
mates. Get her nose out of her books for a while. She's a
good girl.

Brian   I can't.

Father   Now I'll tell you things you've never heard me
talk about. Secrets I keep from Irene. I've seen it. Tanks
on fire. Human ovens. Legs and arms sticking out the
turrets – waving about – like the legs of a beetle on its
back. They were dead – bodies contracting in the heat. We
called it the fire dance. They didn't feel it but we had to
see it. A cannibal would walk away from that with my
blessing . . . You're in a state of shock. I can see it. Ill.
That's why you've got to go to the authorities. If you cut
your finger you go and get it bound up. That's what
authority's for. You don't start barging into little girls'
rooms and telling them the world doesn't understand you
(*Sigh.*) – if you do that you'll be in very deep water my
friend. I'll call the police – for your own sake. If you've got
anything to say to me say it before – (*Stops, puzzled. Stares at*
Brian.) What is it?

Brian   (*starts to laugh*)   . . . the turrets . . .

Father   (*gently, hand on* **Brian**'s *arm*)   I'm sorry you take
the –

Brian   Don't. (*He stands.*) Don't! Questions! Questions!
Prying! You're not happy till you get to – find someone
suffering! What made you like that? You've no right to
question me!

Father   (*low threat*)   Don't look at me like that. No right? –
in my house! No right! If you look at me like that I'll put
your eyes out! My God I'm not a man of violence! I could
take you outside and give you the thrashing of your life!
You couldn't run anywhere, you couldn't crawl! You're

younger than me, but what I feel now – I'd put you down!
. . . I didn't know I could be so angry! What right've you
got to upset me? Did I come here with accusations? I
offered help! D'you think I'll got down on my knees?
Prying? He comes in here taking over my house! I don't
care what you've done! I wouldn't listen if you told me!
You're not important enough to bother with! Keep your
grubby little secret! You're a coward! – that's what you
can't tell!

The door opens and **Irene** *comes in.*

I told you to wait down there!

Irene *goes to* **Brian**.

Brian (*to* **Father**)   I can't tell you! (*To* **Irene**.) How can I
tell it here – to a man like that! In this room – it doesn't
make sense!

Father (*to* **Irene**)   Go down! (*To* **Brian**.) What's wrong
with the room? My God – he doesn't like the wallpaper!
He doesn't like me – the way I live – he doesn't like
anything! (*To* **Irene**.) Go! He was going to tell me – I had
him there – and you barge in!

Brian   Let her alone! You make it worse! – everything
you do! If I wanted to tell you I couldn't now! Look – no
one else knows I'm here! I won't tell! Is that what you're
afraid of? You're in the clear with the –

Father   I beg your pardon? In the clear? I *am* in the clear
lad! Don't patronise *me*! I don't need assurances from you!

Brian (*to* **Irene**)   You told *him*? Trusted *him*?

Father   Now start on her! Get one thing straight: I'm
answerable to no one in this house! What I do in this place
is right because I say so! Oh I'm not letting a little
runaway-sneak like you upset me. I said I'd help you and I
will! I keep my word! It's time you were taught a lesson!
When you leave this house the police'll be on your tail.
Then God help you!

Irene (*to* **Brian**)   You must tell us! There must be
something if it causes all this trouble even before we know
what it is! The police will come – and if there's something
that should be done, we can't do it . . . it'll be too late . . .

Father *goes to the door and opens it.*

Father   Take my advice and move! I'm calling them.

Irene   No! He must tell us what happened!

Father   Nothing happened! (*To* **Brian**.) You've run into
something you can't push out of your way! It's all right
Irene. He saw a few bodies – a *lot*! – saw them dying! (*He
half turns to* **Brian**.) I'm not the fool he thinks I am. I know
what he means about this room. You don't talk about that
here. One day you find yourself somewhere counting
bodies. Well – *someone* wants to know. He wants to go on
counting marbles! Play truant from war! (*To* **Brian**.) What
about the other lads? Did they run? They didn't like it any
more than you. Some of them are dead because you ran!
My God if those lads were out there I'd have to stop them
getting at you! (*He is standing in the open doorway. He bangs his
fist on the outside of the door.*) That's them! Trying to get in!
(*He bangs on the door. He pretends to shout to soldiers in the
corridor.*) All right lads I'll fix him! (*To* **Brian**.) They're not
a pretty sight! (*He comes into the room.*) I'm not leaving you
with my daughter! Get down there!

Brian *takes the gun from under the pillow. He holds it up but does
not aim it directly at* **Father**.

Father (*jeering in fear*)   . . . Oh put it away sonny. You
don't know what you're doing. Now he's got his toys
out . . .

Brian (*shuts the door*)   . . . Oh Christ I didn't want it . . .

Father (*his fear becomes real*)   Put it down son. Put it down.
You don't mean it. That's right – you don't want to
harm –

Brian   Why did he bang on the door! Who are you to let
people in and out just because they're dead.

Father (*mumbles in panic*)   He's mad he's mad oh God why did I try to help the –

Brian   The keeper of the door! Don't call me lad! I'm not your son!

Father   If there was some other way to bring children into the world we would take the care of – please please don't lad – sir – you're harming yourself by – son I –

Brian   Son! Son! He's said it again! If I was your father son! – I'd tell you! – everything! I'd teach you your first word! Say it – say it – after me! *Sorry*! Say it!

Father   Sorry, sorry sorry for everything you – talk to me – I want to help . . . (*Tearful grin.*) . . . Oh is this a game? . . . (*To* **Irene**.) You're in it too . . . !

Brian   The keeper of the door! He saw the dead! In tanks! Dancing!

Father (*panic whisper*)   A madman in our house – shut in with a –

Brian   Get down! Get down! (**Father** *paralysed*.) I told you to get down!

Suddenly **Father** *scuttles to the door.* **Brian** *half trips him.*

No! No! (*Points to floor.*) Down! Down! You don't get out of it now.

Father *drops to his knees.*

Brian (*eyes closed*)   Dance. Like the men in the tank. The keeper of the door. Show me. How they danced in the turret.

Pause.

Father   Err – I – (*He is making a few vague gestures with his hands.*) Sorry.

Brian *has opened his eyes. He stares at* **Father**.

Brian   . . . the pity of it . . . yes . . .

Irene *goes to* **Father** *and helps him to his feet.*

Irene   Get up – you've done enough – there's no need now . . .

Father *head bowed, cringes away from her.*

Father   . . . he'll shoot me with his . . . (*Pushes her away.*)
. . . no no the man will shoot us with the . . . all the people he . . .

Irene   Stand up. (*Lifts* **Father** *to his feet.*) There. No one will hurt you. (*She turns to* **Brian**.) Give it to me.

Brian   Yes . . . take it – take it . . . Let's be at peace.

Brian *gives her the gun. She goes to the desk and sits with it in her lap. Silence.*

Father (*low*)   Ha!

Silence.

He starts to jab the air with his finger. A hollow laugh with each jab.

Ha! Ha! Ha! Ha! Ha! (*Leans against wall.*) A little girl asks – he . . .

Hollow laugh – he sidles with his back along the wall. **Irene** *stands.*

Hahahahahahaha! . . . he gives it! Ha! Ha! Ha! (*Brushes against the picture on the wall, straightens it with one hand.*) The coward afraid what comes – next! Can't go that far! Took in by my little wheeze! Didn't know – took him for a ride! (*Points a finger at the picture.*) 'Colley Wood: A View of the Sea.' (*Suddenly waves his arms as if he's frightening a child by pretending to be a ghoul.*) Oooh! On the run! The only place he runs is in his jeans! It isn't ended, isn't ended! (*He picks up the chair and poses with it menacingly over his head.*) Wouldn't tell? I know now! – what I need! He drew a gun! With witnesses! (*To* **Irene**.) Go down! Get the police! In the street! (*Calls.*) Police! (*To* **Brian**, *still holding the chair as before.*) Stay there! No pity now! It's gone!

Irene   There's no need for the rest.

Father *sharp, jerks head.*

Father   What?

Irene   He came. You came, I came . . . He didn't hurt us
. . . If we knew what we're doing in this room. (*Looks at the
exam papers.*) They want these in the morning. (*To* **Brian**.)
Why can't you tell us what happened? Why not? At least
say that.

Brian *has slumped onto the bed.* **Father** *still stands with the
chair over his head.*

Father (*laugh*)   Write it. Pen and paper.

Irene   I'll go with you.

Father   No you can't. The exams are coming. He'll leave
you. Get you into trouble.

Irene (*to* **Brian**)   How much money have you got?

No answer.

Father   You can't. He doesn't want you. Tell her! It's not
the money! He'd batter some old woman – take you to a
Chinese take-away to celebrate!

Irene   My father hides his money in his room. I'll steal it.

Father   Ha! He's lost his voice – makes a habit! It's the
next day now, the morning after! He doesn't want you!
Pathetic little tart! . . . My daughter's a tart! I'll give him
that: he's got his head screwed on. Wouldn't shoot me: too
messy! Wouldn't take you: cramp his style! See what he is!
You'd go with that? See him! Give him the gun!

Father *puts down the chair, goes to the wall and turns his face to
it.*

Irene *sits in the chair.*

Father   Shoot me! I've turned my back! Made it easy!
Look – I've got a blindfold!

Father *puts the crook of his arm over his eyes, still facing the wall.*

Irene *and* **Brian** *do not move.*

Father   Take the gun! He can't! I could stand here till I drop dead! He can't!

Irene (*to* **Father**)   Don't do it!

Father (*as before, squinting out from under his arm*)   I give the order: shoot!

Irene   Leave him alone. (*Very low.*) Leave yourself alone.

Father (*turns to* **Irene**, *exultant*)   I've never been so safe! I feel it! Every pore!

In the chair, **Irene** *raises the gun – it points at* **Father**.

Irene   Now yes.

Irene *pulls the trigger: click. Silence.*

Father (*too stunned to finish*)   She –

Irene *gets up from the chair. She takes a few steps towards* **Father**. *She is holding out the gun with one hand. The gun shakes violently. She holds it with both hands. The shaking becomes slower but more pronounced. She aims at* **Father**. *He crouches, draws in his breath – almost too high to be heard.*

Irene *pulls the trigger three times: click – click – click. The gun stops shaking.*

Irene   It doesn't work.

Father *scampers across the floor to* **Brian**, *grabs his legs.*

Father (*like a baby being sick*)   She tried to –

Irene (*like a small child*)   It didn't go – I didn't –

Brian *goes to* **Irene**. **Father** *clings and scuttles along behind him.* **Brian** *takes the gun from* **Irene** *– she doesn't resist.* **Father** *scuttles away from* **Brian** *– backs away to the wall.*

Father (*terrified giggle, head in hands*)   I can't – any more –

Brian (*holding out the gun*)   It's not loaded.

Brian *puts the gun on the desk.*

Father *sways to the desk like a cripple. He accidentally knocks a few exam papers to the floor. He picks up the gun, tries to look at it, drops it to the floor. He falls against the desk.*

Brian Brought it to scare anyone who ... I'd never kill ... No bullets – so I'd never be in the situation of...

Father Did she know? Did she know?

Irene *walks to the table.* **Father** *flinches away as she passes.*

Father (*flat whine*) She's got a knife.

Irene *picks up the fallen exam papers. She lays them on the table without sorting them.*

Irene (*looking at the sheaf of papers*) Sometimes there's a terrible tragedy. You have to play your part.

Part Two

Father *and* **Brian** *stare at* **Irene**. *She stares down blankly at the exam papers.*

Father   She tried to kill me.

Brian   She didn't.

Father   My daughter tried to . . . !

Brian   It wasn't loaded – she saw. It's my fault. I brought the gun.

Father   I could be dead. (*He stares at* **Irene**, *then turns to* **Brian**.) Yes your fault! You've done this! You didn't tell . . . ! I never rowed like – we treated each other with respect. Human beings – not animals, criminals! (*He points to the gun on the floor.*) Put it away! Get rid of it!

Brian *picks up the gun.*

Father   She stood there and tried to . . . What am I going to do? I can't live with her here. I can never trust her after what happened in this room. Every cup of tea – I'd wonder what she'd put in it. This isn't my house any more. (*Starts to go.*)

Brian   Where are you going?

Father   To be sick. Is that all right? I have to be in this house with filth – at least let me sick it out of my body!

He goes.

Irene   I don't understand how it happened.

Brian   When the police come I'll hand myself in. What else? Everywhere's like this. I'm – I'm no good at living. I ask too much – and that's too little. Why did you do that to him?

Irene   You made him crawl . . . !

Brian It was a trick – scare him – tie him up – get away
– (*Stops.*) I knew it wasn't loaded. He knew – in the back of
his mind – I didn't mean to kill him. I couldn't fake that.
No one can. I saw squaddies' faces when they killed. It was
on your face. If the gun had been loaded he . . . You were
lucky. It's all over. I'm like him. I can't live with you now.
That's what you've turned me into. When you're shot you
don't have time to hear the gun. You're dead too soon.
You don't even feel the bullet. You're too shocked by
what's on the killer's face. You're looking into hell. So you
think you're already dead and in hell for ever. That's how
they spent their last seconds. Without hope. You went one
better. You made him stare at your face while you fumbled
with the trigger. He's trying to sick your face up. He won't.
You've tattooed it on his brain.

Irene You said you meant to go back – till you saw me.
What did I do?

Brian No, forget it. It's all changed. I'm going back.
Think of what you did to *him*.

Irene I want to know. What does it matter to you now
you're going back?

Brian Everyone's in a room like this. I don't know how
we live in it. I'll tell you. I want to know if you can still
understand. It's not much of a story. It was in the desert. A
temporary hold-up. A few days quiet before the order to go
in. Even in war you can slip away. I took a walk in no-
man's-land. The dunes. Covered in long neat rows of little
waves. Beautiful. Then where they were slashed open by
tanks. Machines dragging their graves behind them. I
passed there and went on. It was still. Flat. Sand. Flatter
than the sky. I saw – how far? – a shadow. Black. Dot. A
periscope sticking up from a secret dug-out? No it was a
moving shadow. First I didn't see the thing that made it.
Lost in the heat. Then I saw something white. Walking on
the shadow. A mirage? In war you're in the mirage. I got
closer. A man. A dwarf. Walking on its own shadow. I
should've turned back. Against orders being there. You

must see everything, it's not given to you again. A little
chap walking away. The shadow round its feet. Five? Six?
It wore a white thing. I thought I was silent in the sand.
Sand must make many sounds. He knew them all. It was a
different place for him. He turned and looked straight over
his shoulder. *At* me. No expression – but he saw. I couldn't
shout. I was afraid the sand would hear me and try to bury
me. I pointed my gun. What else could I do? Not in anger.
It was a pointed finger made of metal. He looked over his
shoulder and went on. Didn't hurry. His face didn't change.
I don't know if he was calm. I ran. Fell. The sand was ice
to me. I slid – digging in – trying to get to my feet. In my
eyes and mouth and collar. That was worst. It trickled
down my back as if, as if . . . I shuddered. I reached him.
He went on. Didn't flinch or change his line. The sand
didn't hurt him – I tore it to bits just being there. I
stumbled beside him. Put out my hand. I couldn't touch
him. Speak English? Speeky Iingleesshh? I was crying.
Spitting sand. Tell me, tell me, tell me . . . He didn't
answer. He didn't have the words. He went on. Sometimes
now I speak – ordinary things. Shut the door – more tea –
and there's bits of sand in my mouth. I fell back. Let him
go. I was lost. Crying. The sand was turning to scum –
mud – on my face. He didn't look round. Went on. He
knew I couldn't hurt him. Some of our planes rose up on
the horizon and went down again. The sand was opening
out between us. A child is lifted from its mother – the cord
stretches. It walked away. From its father – mother – us.
Children are meant to cry for food. The cold. The dark.
Alone. For comfort. It walked away. From everyone. We
hate and kill. It had had enough. Children have begun to
walk away from human beings . . . I let it go – to grow up
into one of theirs to kill us. I went back to my unit. Slow –
the desert was a lump of mud stuck to my boots. We got
the order. Went to war. Killed. Then home. Bands.
Streamers. Celebrations. I can't forget the child. I went for
the wrong walk. I met myself.

Irene   You mustn't tell my father. Please. You'd hurt
yourself. He'd never understand. It'd be one of his jokes. It

would crucify you.

Brian Do *you* understand?

Irene Yes. You can't go back. You mustn't.

Brian Ha!

Irene It's dangerous for you.

Brian You've driven me back! When I saw you I
thought: the child could be hers. The world's okay – safe.
Then you took the gun – like all the rest!

Irene No! It was different!

Brian *How?* (*He stares at her for a moment, then turns away.
Anger.*) What's it matter? I met a loony child! Food doesn't
drop out of the sky just because it's in the desert! Some
sappers clearing mines'll find a little skeleton with sand in
its mouth.

Irene He's climbing up in his socks.

Silence. The door opens and **Father** *comes in. He has taken off his
shoes.*

Father I had a sandwich at the job centre. They've got a
little caff section. Lay on my stomach. (*To* **Irene**.) Sorry
sorry . . . you knew it wasn't loaded . . . we're a family . . .
you'd never . . . it's not possible, it doesn't happen. You
pulled my leg. I was confused – worried over you lad – so
I fell for it. I wish *you* were pulling my leg. But you're
telling the truth. Why should you lie to me? The trouble
you've got coming to you.

Brian You phoned the police.

Father Now now. I told you – I was sick. And I had
other things to think of: I still thought Rene had tried to –
(*To* **Irene**.) Sorry sorry. (*To* **Brian**.) When did I have time
to phone? Don't be silly.

Irene He's giving himself up.

Father Oh? What changed your mind? (*To* **Irene**.) I

didn't phone. (*To* **Brian**.) How can I trust the 'latest'? You might change it again on the stairs.

Irene   The police told you to talk to keep him here.

Father   I'm not repeating myself again. If you'd had the sense to tell me why you came here none of this – the row, the gun – would've happened.

Brian (*to* **Irene**)   Shall I tell him?

Irene   No. Why waste your time? He can't understand.

Father   Try me.

Irene (*to* **Brian**)   Go to prison if you want. But I have to live here. I don't want to see any more. Please.

Brian   I must try. He must understand something. Something must get through to him. Mr Briggs – please – sit down.

Father   Are you going to tell me your *secret?*

Brian   Yes yes.

Father *sits on the side of the bed.*

Brian   Listen. There was a hill. They're dug in on the top. We came up firing. Mortars, grenades. Went in. Cleared it out. We were in a space – like a room – so flat you could've laid a carpet – rocks sticking up like bits left of the walls. Their dead on the floor. Their wounded shivering on the rocks. Quiet. The wounded snivelling – the odd sound of fighting – made it quieter. Fags out, lit up. Ping on the rock. We've got a sniper. Then one of theirs – wound in the gut – started to whine for mum. Same word in any language. It gets louder. One of ours – nerves gone – goes over to theirs yelling shut it, shut it – tries sign language with the bayonet. Theirs: mmeeoowwmmuummhhaaa – like a soccer chant. Ours screaming: not words now – warning – orders – reasons – praying – telling how'd-I-know? – a bedtime story to make him stop – on and on – my language – the language I dream in – this language – but I don't know it – screaming – an animal down his throat he's sicking up, it's digging down. Theirs: maahwah – maahwah – maahwah – maahwah! Ours: screaming. Theirs: maahwah – staring in God's face screaming with a bayonet on judgment day – ping that's the sniper – and God screams and puts the bayonet in – in the wounded belly – in the wha-wha – and theirs arms go up as if it wants to embrace – then fall back to its sides – and flap – like wings on a dead bird falling in the sky – and ours stops jabbing – theirs: a bit of blood pops from its mouth and dribbles down its chin – ours mutters as he wipes his bayonet on theirs jacket. God smokes. The fag still in his mouth. Didn't go out. I didn't understand my language.

Father So what was all the fuss for! I knew that's what it was. I could've told you myself. Not the details but the gist. Why couldn't you tell me before? You had a little war, mine was big. Don't blame yourself. And the lad with the bayonet – *he's* not to blame himself. Theirs should've understood: orders are the same in any language. It's us or them. In my war theirs booby-trapped their wounded. Put your hand out with a fag or can of water – bang! – it's blown off. Us or them. You look after your own. Thank God I've got Rene to care for. You'll find the wisdom of that when you settle down.

Irene (*window*) Police car – end of the road! –

Brian – roadblock!

Irene He's waving up the street – they must be blocking the other end!

Father They followed you. That's what I was afraid of. Tip off from the barracks.

Irene (*bewildered*) You must've told them he had a gun!

Father Rene – you make these accusations! I didn't phone! They didn't need my tip off! Did the barracks go to sleep?

Irene (*to* **Brian**) Go through the back!

Father No no Rene don't – that's not helping him! If I'd phoned – it'd be for his sake – to help him! Only for him! (*To* **Brian**.) They'll have men out the back – all over! Go with them like you said. Finish it now. I'll speak up for you. Please –

no more.

Silence. They look towards the window but do not move.

Irene   Quiet.

Brian   They're on the roof.

Irene   If you'd gone I'd've gone with you. I wouldn't let you go alone!

Father   Rene – you make it worse for the poor lad.

Brian   Too late, too late. No one can help me. I went to the wrong place – saw the wrong things. This is the wrong place too. That's it: wrong – everywhere. (*To* **Father**.) You phoned! Admit it! (*Begs.*) At least that! What does it cost you! Why can't he tell me!

Father   You have your secrets, I have mine.

Brian   I could've walked to the station. Looked in the shops. Seen the sky. No one grabbing my arm.

Father   They wronged you when they put you in uniform. It's not for you. Not fair on the other lads.

The door swings open: half a policeman protrudes.

First PC   Drop your gun!

Brian *turns to the door – sees* **First PC**.

Brian   No.

A shot. **Brian** *drops his gun. He stares at* **First PC**.

First PC   Hands up hands up hands up hands up hands up hands up!

Voices (*outside*)   Hands up hands up!

Brian *backs to the wall, stops when he reaches it. Silence. He lifts his hand. He puts his hand inside his windcheater.*

A shot.

Brian*'s hand comes out of his windcheater – it shakes violently, red.* **Brian** *stares at the shaking hand. It sprinkles him with blood. Outside,* *voices gasp like a circus crowd. Silence.*

Brian   Let me live. Let me live.

Suddenly the whole chest of his shirt is soaked in blood. He slips down the wall – leaving a red smear on it.

*Immediately **First PC** takes enormous strides into the room. An alsation lollops after him. Then a crowd of **Policemen** rushes in. They are misshapen, lumpen: armouring under their tunics. The **Policemen** stand in a half-circle aiming guns at **Brian**.*

Second PC   Watch – watch – trick – feign –

Pause.

Second PC   Search! Search! – Medics!

*Chaos. The **Policemen** scatter and search the room. Shouts, walkie-talkies, barking. Two uniformed legs descending in the window – **Fourth PC** coming down from the roof. **Father** flat against wall. **Medics** with equipment enter.*

First Medic   What's his name?

Second PC   Brian!

Third PC *is holding **Brian** to the floor.*

Fourth PC (*shouts down to the street through the window*)   Ambulance – here – up – he's down – bagged!

Voice (*from the roof*)   Two shots!

Fourth PC (*shouting up*)   Ours!

The room – even more crowded. Medics. Stretcher. Oxygen and emergency equipment. The bed is upended. From outside the sound of police car and ambulance sirens.

First Medic *puts the oxygen mask on **Brian**'s face. In the chaos the alsatian licks blood from **Brian**'s hand. Only **Father** sees it. **Second PC** stands astride **Brian**'s gun on the floor – he has chalk and a tape-measure.*

Second PC   Mind – gun – want it right!

*A **Neighbour** enters with a young **Child** on her arm. A foot strikes* *the gun – it skews towards* **Brian** *and ends up by his hand.* **First Medic** *is adjusting the oxygen mask on* **Brian**'s *face. He stops, stares – at* **Brian**'s *hand as it folds round the gun.* **First Medic** *begins to back away. Slowly* **Brian**'s *arm rises – the gun swings loose in his hand –* **Policemen, Medics,** *the* **Neighbour, Father** *stop – stare – slowly back away to the far side of the room.* **Brian**'s *hand still slowly rises with the gun. His face is blank, livid white and partly hidden by the oxygen mask. Silence except for noise in the street. Some of the* **Policemen** *shyly raise their guns. They stare at* **Brian**. **Fourth PC** *crouches in the open window. The alsatian cowers and whimpers. Pause.*

The **Child** *climbs down from the* **Neighbour**'s *arms. It crosses the space between the others and* **Brian**. *When it reaches him it stops. It chuckles and points its stubby finger at the gun. It turns to face the others. They stare back in silence.*

Child   Look he give them – man give them –

Pause. Suddenly the **Neighbour** *runs forwards, picks up her* **Child** *and runs back with it to the others.*

Neighbour   Naughty – naughty – naughty –

Pause. The gun is slowly slipping through **Brian**'s *hand. It falls to the ground. The empty hand stays in the air, the fingers trying to grasp. The crowd lets out its breath.* **Second PC** *runs to* **Brian**, *throws himself on him, pinioning him to the ground, tears off the oxygen mask and hisses into his face.*

Second PC   Yes? Yes? Yes?

The other **Policemen** *charge forward and pull* **Second PC** *off* **Brian**. *They start to scuffle amongst themselves. The* **Medics** *replace the oxygen mask and attend to* **Brian**. *Unseen by the others a* **Senior Police Officer** *has entered. He stares at the scuffle and then turns on the* **Neighbour**.

Senior Officer   Madam get out!

All the other **Policemen** *suddenly turn to look at* **Senior Officer**. *Moment's pause.*

Neighbour (*to* **Senior Officer**)   Know him – umpteen times – communal stairs – I'm a named witness –

The **Child** *awkwardly pats the* **Neighbour***'s face with its fat little hands trying to gain attention.*

Child   He give mummy – man give them –

Senior Officer (*furious*)   Get out madam. (*Shouts through door.*) Who let this woman in? Put someone on the stairs! It's a sideshow! Chrissake give me some order!

The **Neighbour** *tries to speak to* **Irene** *and* **Father***. She drops her shopping.* **Policemen** *pick it up for her and bundle her out. As she goes she calls back to* **Irene** *and* **Father***.*

Neighbour   Are you all right? Anything you need?

Irene *stands at the table. Her eyes are shut and her hands are flat on the table top: it vibrates. She could be a clairvoyant in a trance. A chain-and-bar ladder suspended from the roof swings like a pendulum over the window.*

Fourth PC (*to* **Irene**)   Are you all right miss?

Irene*'s hands are still on the vibrating table top. Outside, sirens and cars coming and going.*

Fourth PC   Miss? Miss?

Part Three

The room milling with **Policemen** *and* **Medics**. **Brian** – *the oxygen mask on his face, a* **Medic** *injects his arm*. **Father** *wanders trying to find someone to talk to*. **Irene** *stands at the table as before – her hands flat on the table top*.

Fourth PC (*to* **Irene**) No harm now miss. It's over. I'll get a woman constable to attend to you.

The **Senior Officer** *is talking to* **First PC**.

First PC Pointed straight at me.

Senior Officer The second shot.

First PC Hand in his jacket – spoke couldn't make out what – swore straight at me – even when he was down. (*Turns to* **Second PC**.) You saw him with the gun.

Senior Officer (*pauses silently in suspicion, then turns to his second-in-command*) The ammunition could be cached up anywhere – they always have more than one weapon – coming here regularly – the girl wouldn't think – he'd hide it unbeknownst.

First PC Sir can a message be got to my wife and kids? – in case there's any rumours.

Senior Officer His regiment's checking what's missing. (*Turns to* **First PC**.) Good man.

First Medic *checks the oxygen mask on* **Brian**'s *face*.

Senior Officer *goes out to report*. **Second** *and* **Fourth PC**s *stare at* **Brian** *and the* **Medics**.

Fourth PC (*to* **First Medic**) Giving oxygen to butcher's meat.

Fourth PC *goes to* **Father**.

Fourth PC (*to* **Father**) You're being attended to sir. Your statement'll be taken at the station. Would you like to accompany the young lady downstairs? I presume that is your room sir is it? This sight'll upset her.

Father *wanders, trying to find someone to listen to him.*

Father   I warned them he was unstable. I saw his hand go in his jacket. How's your man to know? I'll put it in my statement. Quick reactions you lads. You know your job.

Second PC   In a minute sir!

Father (*goes to* **Irene**)   They're giving him the best attention . . . I knew this would happen. I had to call them: you can see he was out of control. The room could be full of bodies. If you'd let me call them before . . . A gun in a room like this – it takes over. You let yourself in your front door and five minutes later the world's turned upside down. (*He looks at* **Brian**. *Fear.*) That could be me . . . We'll get you another room to sleep in for tonight. It won't be easy to get back to normal tomorrow. God knows what it'll do to your exams.

Irene   I thought the gun had bullets in it.

Father (*half attention, staring at* **Brian**)   No no you're still in shock.

Irene   I thought the gun had bullets in it.

Father   Of course you didn't. How could you tell? You don't know the first thing about guns. Can't even pull the trigger. It was the novelty of it: a gun in your hand – you were upset – so – . Now you feel guilty, accusing yourself for nothing.

Irene   I thought the gun had bullets in it: he said he'd shoot you.

Father   No more. Please. I've had enough. I don't want to hear . . . You don't know *what* you thought. I've told you what happened. That's good enough for both of us . . . Let's go downstairs. I'll take you down. (*He stares at her.*) We're in enough trouble without this. (*Edge of craftiness.*) Anyone who had the nerve to try to kill would be smart enough to shut up about it in a room full of law. – You're a good girl trying to be too honest. It's natural you're confused.

Irene I tried to kill you.

Father (*compassion*) Poor Irene. (*Slight pause.*) You see it yourself: who knows what they do half the time? The policeman *thought* the lad was going to shoot him. He wasn't. And you think you tried to kill me. No no you lost your temper – for a tiny bit of a second. And luck has it there's a gun in your hand. If it'd been a cup you'd've thrown it. Instead you pulled the . . . your luck again: no bullets. A little tantrum doesn't mean you're a killer. Hardly meditated was it? We mustn't even think it could happen. What would it lead to? If we all judged ourselves like you, a room like this would turn into . . . (*Slight pause.*) It's like the man with the bayonet: you don't think he meant it? – it meant nothing. It was the situation. (*He stares at her.*) Sometimes I don't know what goes on in your head.

Brian *starts to breathe stertorously. He is being strapped to the stretcher. The* **Medics** *clear his throat with a suction probe. They connect him to a respirator – the hiss of its mechanical breathing is heard till he is taken away.*

Father (*to* **Irene**) Let's go down. This place will need decorating. All new. More expense on top of everything.

Irene I tried to kill you.

Father *stares at her then looks round in fear.*

Father For Chrissake not here . . . (*Silence. Low.*) What are you telling me? You wanted me dead? Me there instead of him? Now? Is that what you want?

Silence. He starts to pull at a shirt button – the second one down from the collar. Tightly sewn. He grinds his teeth and tears it off.

(*Low.*) Take it. Take it. I won't have it on me. You sewed it on. That's where people hang their lockets – chains – pictures they love – (*He puts the button before her on the table.*) Take it. You sit there and tell me these things. Your father.

Take it. I won't have it. You touched it. Take it.

Irene   I don't know now. I tried to kill you. It was right.

Father   Right? Is this a joke? You sit there and tell me it was right? Right? (*Bewildered.*) I don't know, I don't know, I don't know. Is this something I've got to understand? Isn't what you've done enough – now you want to insult me? If I was dead – on that floor – you'd be spitting on what was left? (*Her jerks at his sleeves as if he's brushing off spit.*) Put me under the floorboards? God knows what you'd be getting up to . . . !

Irene   I tried to kill you.

Father   Stop it! You sit in this room and calmly tell me you – ? It's not natural. Not human. He's dead because he got mixed up with you! You killed *him*! I know that! (*Calls.*) Officer!

Third PC   (*crouched by* **Brian**. *Looks up*)   It's all right sir we're doing all we can. (*Turns back to* **Brian**.)

Father   . . . I don't know what to do. Why have I got to cope with this? You're not well. You need attention. For your own sake. You could do terrible things. You must be put away. You sit there – all the time – day after day – fill in their papers: what's the use? How d'you answer their questions? What's two and two? I tried to murder my father. What's the – capital of Zambia? I tried to murder my father. Is that your world? Nothing makes sense any more. I don't know who we are . . . I don't care if it's true or not! If you can *think* it, it's as bad! Sometimes I'm not a good father. I lose my temper. Rage. No job. I can't give you the authority of a father behind you. But do I deserve this? I tried to make up for my faults. I loved you. I loved you. Took care of you.

Irene   I tried to kill you.

Father   She keeps saying it! Is it a curse? What d'you want me to do? Why are you telling me?

Irene   I tried to kill you.

Father No no – I can't believe it. Never. Something
happened to you – now you're scared – in a state. Are you
trying to drive me mad? Is this the return I get? For a
father's love? No. You're clinging to what happened as if
this stubbornness justified it – was some way out. You're
lost – you'll destroy yourself. We must stop now. Tomorrow
will be different – if you get it right *now*. You understand?
Do it. Show me you understand that – want it – *now*. Then
you're not sick. I'll be content – let it drop. It can go on as
before: life – this house – can go on. We'll be wiser, have
more sympathy for all the little things that – . Start a new
way. No need to bring authority in. Do it on our own. All
you have to do is say you're sorry.

Irene (*immediately*) No. (*Pause.*)

Father She wants to pull all the buttons off! Then laugh!
Spit on me without these clothes! Write in it with her
finger! Then lick it to taste my pain . . . Tell me you're
sorry. For this. What you see now.

Irene No.

Father You will say it. I won't take less. If you're not
sorry I'll open the ground under your feet and push you in!
They won't need to dig a hole. I'm waiting.

Irene No.

Father I shan't wait long. I don't want to know what's in
your head. I don't want to understand. Knowing what you
are would damage me! Just say that word that's all. We'll
live by the rules. That's all you can offer. (*Harsh.*)
Something better may come of it. I hope so. Then we'll
welcome it.

Irene I'm sorry.

Father No. You're not. You say that to prove you're not.
That's the old answer: I murdered my father.

Irene I'm sorry I'm not a better daughter. I'm sorry I
leave clothes on the chairs. I'm sorry I put the lights on.
I'm sorry I don't study enough. I'm sorry I play the radio

loud. I'm sorry you haven't got a job. I'm sorry all day.
I'm sorry the world's what it is – and you've always been
unhappy. I'm sorry he's dying.

*The sounds of medical machines and from time to time the engines
and sirens of cars in the street. The* **Second PC** *chalks a line on
the floor round the shape of* **Brian***'s body. From time to time other*
Policemen *come and go.*

Father   All right. I thought father and daughter were
close. When I was at the end of your gun I was closer to
you. I admit it: you tried to kill me. I saw it in your eyes.
Plain. They were more dead than the hole in the end of
your gun. You had three eyes: they all wanted me dead.
Yours more than the gun's, if the truth be told ... I'm
putting the button in my top pocket – see? – for you to
sew on later when I put it out with the wash. It won't get
lost. Mind you don't put it in the machine. They're hard
on buttons. Break them ... It's over, over, in the past. In a
way you've set me free. Now there's nothing to pretend.
We must go on. I have to live with you. There's still the
problem of my job ... I'm glad you're sorry for the other
things. Now tell me you're sorry for today.

Irene   No.

Father (*begging. Flat*)   Please Irene.

Irene   I can't.

Father (*withdrawn*)   I'm beaten. You can see. I need you
to tell me. Some reassurance. To help me to go on. I've
been like this for years. End of the tether. Before you were
born. I'm at the end. (*Sees his hands.*) I must cut my nails.
Oh Christ. (*Pause.*) I'm glad I'm not your child: I couldn't
live in this world then.

The room seems almost empty. A few **Policemen** *and* **Medics**
are left. **Brian** *is carried out on the stretcher. The oxygen mask
covers his face.*

First Medic (*explaining to* **Father**)   Get the lad to another
machine.

Fourth PC (*turning in the doorway to* **Father**) Best here now. Crowded down there. I'll send the lady up.

Fourth PC *goes out and shuts the door.* **Father** *and* **Irene** *are alone. He gets up and wanders to the wall where* **Brian** *fell. The chalk outline of* **Brian**'s *body on the floor.* **Father** *gazes down — he is standing in the chalk outline. He crouches in the place where* **Brian** *fell when he slid down the wall, but with his forehead against the wall and his back to the room.*

Father They're never sorry. She said I'll take his money. He hides it in a suitcase. If I was dead they'd spend it now. Their loot. She isn't sorry. It's not in her.

He turns to face the room, still crouching. He picks up a broken end of chalk. He draws a line round his feet — the shape of his soles pressed to the ground.

They won't like it. The powers that be. Dead people mustn't draw themselves. Anti the regulations on the use of chalk. This little piggy. I used to have a mother. Open the window if someone's there. This room smells of hospital.

Irene (*opens the window*) I had to tell you. I wasn't angry. I can't tell you why I did it. I don't know the words: no one taught them to me.

Father No more. (*Head on knees, peers up sideways, half-leering, half-crying.*) If I kill myself tomorrow . . . will you be sorry?

Irene It's your life. Do what you want. I'm not to blame. You shouldn't kill yourself.

Father (*stands*) Parents – children – say these things to each other . . . (*He gives a vague, loose kick over the chalk outline.*) I'm glad they shot the little coward . . . little bastard . . . let him rot in hell . . . in his room full of guns . . . (*He goes out.*)

Irene *is alone. She shivers at the open window. She goes to the bed. She takes a grey blanket from it and wraps it round herself. She stands huddled with her back to the door.*

The door opens. A **WPC** *comes in. She is in her late twenties,* *blonde, and ultra smart in an immaculate, close-fitting uniform. She has a shoulder bag. She looks at* **Irene***'s back and sees a huddled crone.*

WPC (*unsure*) Are you the daughter Irene?

Irene *remains huddled, talking half to herself and half to the room. She is still shivering. Her face is livid and grey with weariness.*

WPC No wonder you're cold. (*She closes the window.*) I've been detailed to look after you. A car will take us to the station. We've got a comfort room. You must see a doctor.

Irene *mumbles a few words to herself. Tiredness has lowered and broken her voice.*

WPC You've had an ordeal.

Irene He gave it to me. It was in my hand. I looked down at it . . . I've been so confused. They teach you this and that. I try to understand. Their confusion. They say it's a map. It's nothing, blank. Then I looked down – and the paper turned over – I saw – suddenly – clearly – the map's on the other side. I understood. There is a right and wrong, some things shouldn't be. It was right. Then. To do it. So I did. I pulled the trigger. And there were no bullets – I can't be touched. It's done. Now. Always. It's mine. I understood . . . it won't be like this all the time. The confusion will come back – it's outside the door!

WPC They'll give you a social worker.

Irene *stumbles slightly, shakes violently.*

Irene Food in the freezer – sew the buttons – in and out – crying – shouting – yah yah yah – (*Pulls the blanket tighter. The shaking changes to a tremble.*) But I saw. For a moment. I understood. I did it. It's mine. Always. When I'm old – look back – remember the people in the room – I'm sorry people are unhappy – but it will be different then – it will change – I know – it will be mine too – they will change.

WPC (*trying to understand. Glances at the papers on the table*) You're studying for your exams?

Irene   ... when I'm old...

WPC (*craning her neck forward*)   Pardon I didn't hear.

Irene (*as before*)   ... when I'm old...

WPC   You'll have to speak up if you expect me to hear.

Irene *looks up. She has hardly been aware of the* **WPC**. *She stares at her, raises her voice a little.*

Irene   ... there was a child ... it walked ... (*Slightly louder.*) ... walked ...

WPC   A child walked?

Irene (*looks down*)   Away. (*Silence.*)

WPC   A lost child? You mustn't upset yourself any more today. You can't be responsible for everything. Someone's found it. Taken it to the station. It's home by now.

Irene (*blunt*)   The war. (*Twists round to face* **WPC**.) War.

WPC (*puzzled for a moment. Realises, guesses*)   Ah – *he* told you – ? They provide for orphans. The Welfare Authorities – Red Cross. They place them with families now. After they've been vetted and matched. They're very thorough. I bet it's in bliss. Children know how to cater for themselves. They make the most of what's on offer. (*No response.*) He died in the hall. Don't blame yourself. It's going to be all right. People get over worse. You don't believe me but I've seen it. What's wrong with your voice?

Irene *looks at her. Then she goes to her, stops when she is close and gazes into her face.*

WPC (*stiff*)   Is anything the matter dear?

Irene   Poor woman. Poor woman.

WPC (*drawing back, half-embarrassed, half-threatening*)   Don't do that.

Irene's *hand goes out to a plastic bottle of cosmetics on the table. She picks it up and thrusts it at the* **WPC**.

WPC It's yours. Don't you want it?

Irene Take it.

WPC *takes the bottle.* **Irene** *turns and walks away. Stops.*

Irene ... there's sand in my mouth ... scraping my gums ... the little boy's dead – the sand scraping his little bones ... scraping the wind ... Why? Why? Why?

WPC (*looking at the plastic bottle*) Good firm. (*Holds it up.*) Are you sure you don't need it?

Irene (*to herself*) What day is it? I must lie down now. Sleep. Now. Tomorrow.

She lies on the bed, still wrapped in the blanket. She is young again. The **WPC** *stands guard at the window.*

Irene Let me live. Let me live. (*She falls asleep.*)

The Rehearsals
The Dramatic Child
Famine

'The Rehearsals' was written for the Royal Court Theatre revivals of *Saved* and *The Pope's Wedding* in 1984.

'The Dramatic Child' was written for the Founding Conference of the International Drama and Education Association, held in Portugal in July 1992.

'Famine' was written for a benefit evening in aid of the former Yugoslavia held at the Duke's Playhouse, Lancaster, in February 1993 and first published as a broadsheet.

The Rehearsals

This story was told to me some years ago. It may be that my memory has forgotten some of the details and my imagination has added others. But the parts which seem untrue are not imagined and what I have forgotten are merely ordinary things that might occur in any story. Perhaps after all I have forgotten nothing. I wish to make this clear before I tell the story because the story is true.

Once upon a time there lived in a village a boy. When he was twelve soldiers came in a lorry and drove away with him and twenty other boys of about his own age, his friends and neighbours. The lorry travelled two days and a night. At regular mealtimes it stopped and the children were given army rations to eat. They arrived at a small town and were told to jump down from the lorry. Then they were formed into ranks and marched under guard to a large old house. It looked like many of the other houses in the town: built to shelter solid, middle-class, late nineteenth-century prosperity. The roof was grey-slated and the over-hang of the eaves at the two side ends was decorated with an ornamental wooden facia. The house had four storeys and, as they later found, a cellar.

The children were marched into the house. Inside were blind people seated on chairs in rows round the sides of the rooms with their backs flush against the walls or gathered into groups in the middle of the rooms. Others sat in the corridors or lay in beds or on the floors. A few sat on the sides of the stairways. There were no empty chairs. Perhaps there had been a store of them and one had been issued to each blind person as they arrived until the store was empty. The only people in the house who could see were the boys and their guards and a few orderlies.

The boys were told to wait. Almost immediately an official came into the house from the street. He wore a grey suit, an old, greasy, dark tie and an armband. He carried a stack of scripts. From his voice the children knew that unlike the soldiers he belonged to their own nation. He told them they were to rehearse a play which later they would act to a group of visitors. They were to begin work immediately. The children were pleased to have a play to act. They handed out the scripts among themselves and started to organise rehearsals. The blind people were silent. They did not speak to each other or question the children. The old ones did not even speak to themselves. All the same it was difficult to rehearse with them there. They crowded the rooms and as the actors were still only children no doubt they wished to put a lot of running and jumping about into the play. They explained their difficulty to the guards. The NCO went off to see the official with the armband. After fifteen minutes the NCO came back. The official had said the rehearsals were to take place in the attic. They found this to be a spacious room running the whole length of the house. It was well lit from studio lights in the sloping ceiling and from electric lamps. But the floor was covered by dead bodies and so again there was a problem of finding sufficient free space in which to rehearse. The NCO had said that the official had said the bodies were to be taken down to the cellar. As the play was to be performed in a few days, rehearsal time was short and so the children were not permitted to waste any in carrying the bodies down to the cellar. Instead the soldiers collected a gang of blind people to do this. It was the sort of non-demanding work they could manage. It was only necessary for the soldiers to stand one blind person at the head of each corpse and another at the feet. Then order them to stoop, grasp the head or ankles and move forward. The soldiers organised a file of pairs of blind people each carrying a corpse and led them from the attic, winding their way on the staircase round and round down through the house to the cellar while up in the attic the children got on with the rehearsal of the play.

And the children enjoyed rehearsing it and later acting it to the visitors. They couldn't understand the visitors' language and noticed that some of them even seemed to be speaking to the others in a language which was not their own so that they stumbled over words and used more elaborate gestures than they would normally have done. Children are very observant. All the same the play must have been well received: if it had not been they would have been told. And surely watching children act is always a pleasure?

Many of the things in this story may seem strange to us. It might seem strange to gather all the blind people from a wide area and put them together in one house. Wouldn't they have been better off and happier spread among the seeing community? It also seems strange that the attic should have been full of bodies. And strange that soldiers should herd together children and take them away from their homes and families. But none of these things seemed strange to the children. On the contrary they expected these and similar things to happen. It was what their experience of the world and indeed their learning had taught them to expect as natural. And they were very pleased to be taking part in a play. I do not know what it was called.

Later most of the children were killed by being forced to breathe gas. This also may come to seem normal to some people in some places. One of the children was not killed but survived in ways and for reasons that are of no relevance to this story. Many years later when he was well into middle age and indeed on the threshold of becoming old he was walking in a street in New York. He was not thinking about his childhood or, as he recalls, of anything very much at all – when suddenly he burst into tears. He stood where he was in the street, buried his face in his hands and his howls were heard above the noisy traffic of a metropolis. He had suddenly realised that the events in this story in which he had taken part were strange.

Edward Bond
1984

The Dramatic Child

To whom may a child bear witness? To bear witness a child must itself be an authority. It has noticed something and intelligibly recounts what it has noticed. But it will give its account to another authority – to someone or others – who understand the account and who will act on it. This bridges the chasm between self and society. In bearing witness a child seeks understanding and justice. It tries to learn the values that give order to the world. To educate a child means to enable it to bear witness to its life.

There are two widely accepted – but false – beliefs concerning the upbringing of children. Really they are negative and positive versions of the same argument. The negative version is that a firmly disciplined child will grow to be a decent, law-abiding citizen; but a child will grow to be antisocial if its parents are not strict enough with it. A child trained in fear may conform – but fear produces obedience without the ability to judge, or cynicism with the inclination to opportunism. And obedience is the moralised form of cynicism.

The positive version of the argument is that a child loved and given security grows to be responsive, humane, considerate of others and able to act for a shared good. This version has clear advantages over the negative version. But it is not true that love and care enable a child to grow to be happy and considerate. It may become idly content – not given to brutal obedience but nevertheless unable to protect itself in a bad society.

Both these sorts of education do not develop the child's capacity to be critical. Above all, they do not allow the child to enter creatively into the drama and tensions of its psyche.

It is necessary, here, to anticipate the end of the argument. Our present society changes rapidly and substantially. People need to become responsible for change, to understand and evaluate it and when possible to initiate it by anticipating necessity. Children must be helped to make change more human. To become competent members of a critical culture.

This cannot be done by discipline, love or information alone – the child must enter with authority into its self-drama or become its own victim.

We need to understand what culture is – and our present cultural state. Western culture is replacing other cultures. Other cultures are as endangered as other species. In the past all cultures had to do two things: provide the means of existence and explain the meaning of existence – bear witness to life. The two things are closely connected. The economic and technological means of existence depended on forms of social organisation and ownership. These forms were necessarily also the authority that decreed the meaning of existence. A society's culture is the explanation it gives of itself. As human life is not static, culture had to maintain stability but also accommodate and legitimise change. When it could not, change was reactionary or revolutionary. All cultures had to accommodate conflict and tension or be changed by their inability to do so. Otherwise they could not provide the means of existence.

A child's natural state in society is conflictual. Its relation to the world is critical. It lives in a state of change, a dynamic flux which finds direction only by bearing witness. A child's psyche resembles society in its structural instability. This is not fortuitous. If it were not so we would live in evolutionary time and not in history. History happens because we are born in ignorance and have no instinctual place in society. Society is not a projection of instincts. Culture is an artificial, necessary contrivance. For history, technology (and its logic of development) are what chance and genetic mutation are to natural evolution.

A child's conflictual nature is not an extension of animal aggression. Indeed, it is our 'aggression' which prevents us from being animals. A child's conflicts are always a struggle over ideas, over the meaning of its self and of life. Animal aggression is always the attempt to maintain the status quo, to stabilise the state of the species. All human conflict is an effort to impose a new meaning on the world or to respond with new meanings to changes imposed by new technology. Again, this is analogous to the child's state. For a child, parents and other authorities are like the arrival of technology from the future; they impose new situations and demands (as technology does on the community) and the child must retain the integrity of its psyche yet constantly recreate itself in relation to these changes. This is the process of growing up. To the child, education is what history is to society – a means of recording and evaluating events so as to create a culture or character. However caring it is, the relationship between, on the one hand, a child, and on the other its parents and society, must be conflictual – just as history must. It might be possible for societies to create institutions that removed conflict from history, but the relationship of child and authority will always be conflictual – a strife of ideas – because children have no institutions. Children face the raw paradoxes of growing amongst signs of decay, of the weak among the strong. They become healthy by achieving wounds. This belongs to the drama of self that takes place in the social theatre.

Animals may depend on aggression because evolution (unlike history) is not the arbitration of ideas. Animal aggression is always mindless, action at the behest of instinct. Humans are never aggressive because even their violent conflicts are always an arbitration of meanings, the imposition of new meanings or the adaptation to old ones. The meanings are either the psyche's direct expressions or the responses to society's cultural meanings. These become part of the psyche, the way life is (or should be) lived. Though human conflict is a struggle for reason, it does not follow that meaning can always be arbitrated by reason. This is because cultural ideas are embodied in living practice with emotional and physical cognates. But (I repeat because it is important) this is not a human adaptation of animal instinct. Conflict divides us from prehuman animals and makes us creatures of cultures and ideas. We may call ourselves creatures but not animals because we are embodiments of our mind and we live our culture and its inevitable tensions.

It is important to understand the child's conflictual state. It has a will but it is not conceded autonomy and authority. Its mind is devoted to understanding the world – and its basic philosophical riddles – yet it does not have intellectual means to understand the world's structures and social relationships. It urgently needs evaluation but cannot wait for the facts. It cannot understand the world's dystopia. Essentially the child is bearing witness – recording the facts and seeking meaning for them. Many of the conflicts in the child's development have counterparts in society and history. The child must maintain its existence in a world others own. It lives on the sufferance of its good behaviour. It seeks understanding and meaning yet is in conflict with the forms of ownership that decree meaning. It asserts and adapts its will in order to become owner of itself. In societies this search for self becomes generalised, by the pressures of co-operation, into the development of democracy – and as time passes it gives new meanings to the word.

Achieving the means of subsistence requires social ownership, and ownership of the means entails ownership of ideas and cultural ends. Yet all cultures are conflictual because society cannot fully represent the manifold psyches of its members: their roles are in conflict. And even if it could, the condition of childhood would make the adult psyche a source of conflict.

Culture justifies the ways in which the means of subsistence are organised and owned and in doing so humanises existence, whether an existence of poverty or privilege. Paradoxically this does not mean that with the passing of time our actions become less barbarous. Our barbarism 'shrinks' but increasing technological power gives greater expression to the remnant. It is conceivable that when our species is at its most 'humane' its activities will be at their most barbarous and destructive. That is a paradox of modern technological civilisation. When the paradox is misunderstood it feeds back as the despair of 'high culture'.

Is Western society the highest form of humanisation yet achieved and is that why it erases other cultures? For a time Western affluence provides the means of existence more abundantly than traditional cultures can. But all cultures need ideas which justify their economic systems and which (in doing so) humanise culture and psyche. The social means of existence can only be maintained by humanising culture. But this is no longer so for Western affluence – and that is comparable to a major mutation in our species. In the West it is no longer necessary to create a culture and the ideas which humanise and give meaning to life – it is only necessary to maintain a system: the system of manufacturing, markets and money. Western societies are the first human societies that have dispensed with the making of culture. They depend not on their ability to humanise and legitimise authority – but on providing goods. They are societies of means without ends. The system depends on markets and prisons; and more and more of its institutions become types of prisons. Now authority begins to use education to install the prison in the psyche.

These claims are not rhetorical. Western affluence erases other cultures because it is not a culture. It provides goods without the struggles of the psyche to create culture. The psyche's conflicts cannot be erased but authority can co-opt them in intra-social anger and conflict. This reinforces the negative state I have already described – the antisocial conformity of obedience and discipline. Western 'anti-culture' colonises the artefacts and forms of the cultures it erases – but in dehumanised ways, replacing tradition with fashion, development with novelty, solidarity with charity. It assimilates a culture by reversing its meaning – even to those who created it. That is the secret of its power. It turns a force of preservation and adaptation into a force of destruction. Means without ends! The West's economic system is parasitic on the cultures of the past, on the cultures the system destroys. It enslaves whole cultures and works them to death . . . And what it does to other cultures it must inevitably do to its own first source of cultural renewal: children.

Its children have nowhere to turn to bear witness. Their conflicts have no counterparts in adult conflicts. The child seeks meaning, adults struggle to maintain a system. The means have become the ends. Societies' artefacts are, now, not expressions of culture, demonstrations of its meaning, but merely things to consume. Objects lose meaning and become the toys of those who cannot play. Consumption replaces living. And machines think for us. The humanising tendency of the past is reversed. Society begins to become more barbarous.

We should not be nostalgic about the past and its confusions, sufferings, poverty and labour. That is not the alternative. But we live in a dangerous time. There is apparent consumer choice yet the system requires – compared to the past – an inappropriate level of conformity. The system must create inequality and (in any working society) this must create injustice – and in turn social tension. In response authority becomes more authoritarian and intolerant of systematic criticism. America allows free speech but empties words of their meaning. In America you can say everything and it means nothing. Narcotics, violence – even poverty – become sorts of consumer options. Social relations are dehumanised. Democracy becomes a form of tyranny.

That is the story of recent political history. Nonentities achieve great power. They introduce antisocial systems and call them reforms. Their spoken motto is 'there is no society'. Their secret motto is 'there is no culture'. In future – in the time of our children's adulthood – political mavericks will appear from nowhere – or to be precise, from the gutter or the bank. Their simplistic, reactionary programmes will do more damage to society. Then in their fear and anger 'democracies' will elect even more extreme and dangerous pseudo-saviours.

The child's conflictual needs will not be legitimised and developed by education, even in the concealed forms traditionally accepted by cultures. Education will be instrumental, adapting the child to maintaining the system. Conflict has always expressed itself in culture – the struggle over the meaning of 'being human'. Now education will deny a child culture – and thus strive to dehumanise it. The child may (though it may well not) be provided with technological gadgetry – and with the signs and artefacts of many cultures – but only in the superficial way in which the market exploits the exotic.

Education should enable children to search for meaning so that they may bear witness to life. The psyche is a dramatising structure and cultures are in a wide sense theatres. At first the child egoises the world, then anthropomorphises it – and then seeks personal and social meaning. The child becomes a changing, embodied evaluation of the world.

The distinction between sport and art is revealing. Sport has often been of profound importance in culture. Maya ball games were literally a sacred matter of life and death – the losers were sacrificed. Now in the West sport is a matter of neutral skills to which enormous cultural, ideological and national significance is attached. Capitalism could not exist without sport. Sport arbitrates conflict on a fixed field according to fixed rules. It is used instrumentally while appearing to be cultural. This is not to deny the skills of sport and their aesthetic aspects. But mass sport becomes the site of violence precisely because governments and the market cathect it with cultural significance. Football 'hooligans' – even terrace racists – are disputing ideas with authority.

But drama is a game of no fixed rules. The point is to discover and create rules during the drama. Dramatic structures are unlike sport rules because the goals of drama are not defined as they are in sport. Drama searches for meaning and expresses the need to bear witness to life. Drama uses disciplines to define meanings, not take the place of meanings. And culture is essentially dramatic. It uses dramatic processes and expresses itself in dramatic signs. This belongs to the humanising of our species. History and politics are transmitted through the psyche, and so culture is not purely superstructural but is – like the psyche – part of the material basis. When that is understood it can be seen why all culture is conflictual and can only be created in drama, not learned by rote, even when rote is practised as skill. A mind that could not recognise a story (and that means, being part of the story) would be mad. A psyche that cannot dramatise itself (and that means, being an active part of social change) would be a prison. Cultures always contest the division between the real and the imaginary. It is one of the ways societies have access to the material world. Drama is concerned with the tensions of this boundary. In history the imaginary becomes real and the real is consigned to the imaginary. There is conflict between ideology and truth – and even a shared purpose of madness and sanity. If the mind cannot enter – create – the drama of these encounters, the encounters are acted out in the real world of weapons and politics. Drama is not a substitute for politics and does not do away with weapons. But unless our psyches have access to the drama-of-the-boundary, politics goes mad.

Perhaps Western affluence will maintain itself till it comes up against the limits it itself creates. Then it will face the scarcity and inadequacy that have endangered all cultures. In the past cultures had the humanised resources to respond creatively to these dangers. A dehumanised system would not. It would have no creative cultural resources because its 'culture' is parasitic. It could respond only with discipline and violence. So two problems face us. How to protect the world from the market's ravages – and how to protect the chance of cultural renewal and creation that children give us. Their conflictual need creates knowledge and human-value out of our material necessity. Children bear witness to our humanity. We must help them to do this in ways that test and legitimise their conflict or we dehumanise the future. Crises would no longer provoke our strengths but find out our weaknesses and destroy us.

For a time communities may exist without culture. It takes time for their entropy to overcome the dynamic of the past. But no child could exist without a need for culture: it is part of a child's conflictual need. Yet education is so misunderstood that we could use it to kill off the child's need. Whenever that is done we fall into inhumanity and terrible things happen to us. 'Being human' is not an instinctive thing, it is learned in the psyche's drama. The future is threatened by a corpse with a whip. The market's needs do not wholly represent human needs: often they are in conflict with them. Education for the market's needs could be a prison. We must educate children for democracy. The psyche and society are a theatre or they are a prison. At the heart of all democracy is drama.

Edward Bond
1992

Famine

The wind said
Little child in your days
Ten thousand thousand breaths will enter and pass the gate of
   your mouth
I will blow the last breath away
I will scatter it east and west
To the north and south

The wind said
Little child under your skin four thousand bones
Are knit as cunningly as a spider's web
I will pick each bone clean
Like a vulture feeding on dreams
And scatter them in the garbage of war
I will make chaos
Like soldiers sharpening knives on war memorial stones

The wind said
Little child in your mouth are the sounds of a thousand pains
I will blow your shrieks over the city gratings
I will blow your cries over the frozen peaks
I will blow your sobs into the hollow plains

In what scroll is it written you shall die?
Little child I have blown the scroll into the empty sky
I have scattered the books of law
And the charters of state
For your grave I gave you ruins
And for your pall hate
Cities have been laid waste
And armies lie dead
But no one gave you water to drink
Or a crust of bread

Edward Bond
1993

Interview with Edward Bond

and

Teaching Notes for *Tuesday*

Compiled by Jim Mulligan, former Head of English at Pimlico
Comprehensive in London. He is now a freelance writer and
Education Consultant.

Interview with Edward Bond

Tuesday is Edward Bond's second play for television and his first written for young people of 14–17 years.

When he was that age Edward Bond had already left school and was working in factories and warehouses in North London with little indication that he was to become a celebrated and controversial dramatist.

He had been evacuated to Suffolk and Cornwall but finished his formal education at Crouch End Secondary Modern School which he left when he was fifteen.

> I grew up in a world war so things tended to be disorganised, but in many ways it was an education in itself because one learned what it was like to be bombed. I remember little of my education but what left a great impression on me was the personality of the educators.

Some of his teachers were interested in regimentation and he tried to avoid that. The real educators were those who were generous enough to allow him to question. He was born into a traditional working-class culture and his parents, recently moved from the countryside, could not read, so there were no books at home and the books he got in school were:

> boring and patronising, about highwaymen and smugglers and the plays we were given to read, in a very working-class area, were totally remote, about public schools and going into the quad and doing prep.
>
> I did some writing at school and vaguely, at the back of my mind, I thought I wanted to be a writer. I was interested in words and, like most working-class people, was good at talking. Talking is drama so when I wanted a platform to express my ideas it seemed natural to write plays.

At that time all eighteen-year-old men had to do two years' service in the armed forces and this is when Edward Bond really started to write.

> I didn't like what I saw and I wanted to write about it. There was an atmosphere of violence and coercion. It was a

very brutal society. Various ranks were given very unjust powers over other people and if you were an offender you could be publicly humiliated, degraded and brutalised. I saw in it an image of the society outside the army.

Tuesday is a play that deals with the issues that Edward Bond has been writing about for thirty years: authoritarianism in families and society at large, the causes and effects of violence and war, and the impact of these on working-class people.

The play is about a soldier, Brian, who has gone absent without permission after his dreadful experience in a recent desert war. He is tormented by a memory of a small boy he saw in the desert and his memory is entwined with an experience when one of his fellow-soldiers bayonets a prisoner to death. Brian, armed with a gun, seeks refuge in the house of a girlfriend, Irene. She persuades him to give her the weapon and then, suddenly aware of the way her father has oppressed her, Irene attempts to kill him but the gun is not loaded. Her father then telephones the police who, thinking Brian is armed and dangerous, burst in and shoot him.

Edward Bond was asked to write the play by the BBC for the English File series.

I thought about what were the pressing problems and opportunities for young people and this is what I decided on. Obviously it fitted in with what I was writing and where my writing had brought me to. All previous plays prepare you to write the next play. I started working about six months before we filmed in the studio. I remember the story of the little boy who was lost in the desert suddenly popped up one late morning and I thought, yes, that's what I will write about. This is one of the central ideas. You could say there's this little boy in the desert who's running away from his parents. Compare that with the story of the soldier who is screaming for his mother as he gets bayoneted. Compare that with Brian who is shot in the room and compare that with Irene deciding to shoot her father. I want the students to think and feel about these images and compare them to our society.

It is a slow process of getting ideas. I work out very

carefully what I am going to do before I write. I make lots of notes which are at least four or five times longer than the play itself. The actual business of writing always takes me by surprise and things that you thought were not going to be important turn out to be more important. I work every day from ten in the morning until seven in the evening. But, on the last draft, I can work very long hours, sometimes typing throughout the day and the night and I find it a great joy to do that although I don't keep it up for a long while. After the first draft I will do five or six drafts before the play is complete.

Originally I was going to say: the girl has this experience and then, when she's eighty, she looks back and talks about it. And then I thought: if I can't make this experience authentic to an audience in that room at that time then in some way I am not facing up to the problem. So in the end I set the play in one very small room and it all happens in 'real time' of one and a half hours. At the end of it you've got to feel that the girl is completely changed and that her life will be different after that. She has understood things that, at the beginning of the play, she did not understand.

Edward Bond acknowledges the enormous debt he owed as a young writer to George Devine at the Royal Court Theatre and Joan Littlewood at the Theatre Royal Stratford East.

I was just lucky there had been a breakthrough. If I'd been a writer ten years before nobody would have done my plays. Then working-class characters were either comic or part of the sub-plot. But at that time the Royal Court Theatre wanted young writers. The man who ran it, George Devine, said if there was anybody he should get rid of it was me because I would never write anything that could possibly be performed. Despite this he was very helpful. He couldn't understand a word I wrote because his training in theatre was entirely different. And yet, although that was his opinion, he did not base his actions on it.

Despite this support it was touch-and-go whether one of Edward Bond's first plays would be put on. *Saved* had a violent and controversial climax when some disaffected youths stoned a baby in a pram and killed it. When the writer refused to make cuts the play was banned, but still the Court put it on, trying to use a loop-hole in the law. They were fined by the authorities.

Edward Bond says he was surprised by the way *Saved* was criticised.

It would be immoral not to portray violence in plays. I find the mechanical violence in films and TV, the cult of encouraging people to seek personal revenge, very primitive and dangerous. If I show violence, it is always for it to be understood. It is not an end, never a solution. It is always a problem. I take violence and use it in such a way that for once an audience will be able to think about it in the context of the lives they are living and the society they live in.

I don't believe that being non-violent sets an example. You can be a child in the Gulf or somewhere and you can say: I am going to be non-violent. It doesn't stop somebody dropping a bomb on you. How would they know that you had made this remarkable decision? I am very much against war and violence. Violence is never anything other than force and that is very limited. It is never a philosophy, never a thought, but I can see situations where there is very little alternative to using violence. The one thing you can say about it is that it is legitimate when the weak use it against the strong but never the other way round. I was trained as a killer in the army but I have never killed anyone and I don't think I have ever been forced to use violence. When I was young I was exposed to a certain amount of parental violence. It was pretty customary then and I was assaulted by teachers.

When people say to me: you are exposing kids to violence, I say: when they get older they are going to be asked to vote for violence. I think it is legitimate for kids to ask why is it that adults are so violent.

I was once asked to give a talk in Coventry Cathedral, a sermon, I suppose it was. While I was thinking what to say I sat down in a kind of burger-bar. It was a summer evening and the place was full of families with their kids. In the short time that I was there I heard eight people say to children: if you do that again I'll kill you. And nobody paid any attention. I think it is legitimate for children to question that.

I think the future we face may be very bleak and the process of becoming less violent and more peaceful may be reversed. In the nineteenth century more people were beginning to realise that brutality by the state against the individual was a bad thing. It took some time to get there but they knew it was so. Now America is reintroducing the death penalty and the more affluent it becomes the more violent it becomes. My play is against all that.

Another central theme of *Tuesday* is the abuse of authority. In the play Irene has a flash of inspiration when she realises how much she is oppressed by her father and she attempts to kill him. Edward Bond wants this action to be understood.

I want my play to give the audience a sense of the practical, that if you make certain decisions, then you have to stand by them. Irene wouldn't say she was sorry. Her father would say: 'Come on. You don't entertain those thoughts in polite society. You learn to make excuses, to smile, to say the nice thing to authority.' But what Irene in effect says is: 'Actually, no. I don't want to do that because, in the end, if you do those things, you believe them yourself.'

I think, for a moment, she wanted to kill her father. This doesn't mean I want children to go around killing their parents and I don't want parents to go around killing their children even though it happens with astonishing frequency.

To anyone who says: 'Wasn't she lucky there were no bullets in the gun,' I want to say: 'No, wasn't the father lucky.' What I did in the play was apply a little trick. The gun happens to be unloaded but she doesn't know that and the audience doesn't know that. Therefore, the audience can go through this experience, can reflect on it and get new ideas. They can examine their emotions in relation to this thing and that makes the play useful to them. I am not saying: imitate that.

In his search for what will make society a better place to live in, Edward Bond does not see religion as a help.

I was terrorised by religion when I was young. I was told God so loved his son that he killed him. This seemed to be totally perverse. I remember being horrified by it, walking along the road and suddenly shuddering. It seemed bizarre and cruel. I think most children, when they are told this, must be traumatised in some way. It may be that it can be hidden, but religion is learning to be afraid. It is a very cruel idea that somebody should torture and kill somebody in order to save somebody else from something called sin. Murder is murder whether it is done by God or civilians or soldiers.

In recent years some theologians have even said that greed is good, it is good to be acquisitive. This means that we are living a basic conflict. Adults can't live by ten commandments yet children are expected to live by a hundred commandments and adults get upset when the children can't do it. You can't say: we'd like you to be acquisitive *here* but not *there*. It's like saying: we want the river to run in this direction here but will it just turn back there. Once you start releasing energy in a certain way, that's it. People can go to the Stock Exchange and make huge fortunes doing nothing and somebody else is expected to live quietly in apathy and poverty. We make young people cynical. Either they become cynical and opportunistic like many adults or they do what the kid in the desert does – they walk away from us.

Edward Bond would like his play to stimulate questions, to promote coherent thought and to help young people to be autonomous.

My play is written to take young people back to important basic situations and enable them to question what it means to be a human being. Young people ask very profound questions. What is the meaning of life? What is the meaning of the world? But later on they learn to ask how can I survive in my job? How can I pay my mortgage? Do I like my neighbour? The questions tend to get narrower as people get older. But there is a way of stopping this. There is always built into human societies non-conformity or the need to question. Not the need to believe. Lots of people believe mad things. I don't know of any mad questions but beliefs – there are many, many mad beliefs.

Education, at the moment, is trying to teach people not to question and if that happens we become dehumanised. Then the future is very bleak.

With *Tuesday* there are questions but no answers. Edward Bond is inviting the audience and readers to ask questions: the answers have to be worked out in their own lives.

Teaching Notes

I can't tell you why I did it. I don't know the words. No one taught them to me.

The language of this play may seem deceptively simple; there are very few difficult or dialect words. But what makes the text so powerful is that there are no wasted words. Let your attention slip for a few lines and you have missed something important. All the work in this section assumes that you have seen the video of *Tuesday* at least once and you are prepared to study the text so that you can think about some of the questions Edward Bond asks.

What's it all about?

To start with, discuss the following statements with someone. Try to agree on which statement sums up best what *Tuesday* is about and rank the rest of the statements in order of importance.

This play is about:

a) a boyfriend who comes between a father and his daughter
b) a young soldier deserting from the army only to be betrayed to the authorities
c) violence and death
d) a teenager who tries to kill her father
e) the way authority is used or abused in our society
f) people being responsible for their own actions
g) an unexpected violent incident that destroys a loving family
h) two totally unnecessary deaths
i) two young people who want to live but are prevented from doing so
j) a hardworking young woman whose life is ruined by her boyfriend and father

Peeling the onion: layers of meaning

When I'm old – look back – remember the people in the room – I'm sorry people are unhappy

Who is the most influential character in *Tuesday*? Work with somebody to rank the following people in order of importance:

Irene, Brian, Mr Briggs (Irene's father), the boy in the desert, the prisoner who was bayoneted, any other character

At one point Edward Bond thought of putting Irene's mother in the play. What do you think about his decision to leave her out?

Before studying a character you need to make a note of any relevant references or quotations.

Suppose you are going to give a talk on Irene. You might decide to divide your talk into six sections:

- appearance etc.
- relationship with Brian
- relationship with Father
- Father's attitude to her
- Brian's attitude to her
- her new self-knowledge

Your first prompt card might be something like this:
Student
Mid-teens
Dress – skirt, blouse, open cardigan
We don't know what she looks like
Single child in single-parent family. No mother
More than one boyfriend? – *I thought it was her other one*

Prompt card 2: Irene's relationship with Brian
She puts her arms round him
I won't jeer
Was it my letters?
There's no one will hurt you
I'll go with you

Prompt card 3: Irene's relationship with her father
My father hides his money in his room. I'll steal it
You made him stare at your face. He's trying to sick your face up
He's my father. It's his house – implying that the father comes into her room if he wants
I sew buttons on his shirt

Prompt card 4: the father's attitude to Irene
Wait down like a good girl
You're not talking to Rene, even in my presence
Pathetic tart . . . my daughter's a tart
I can never trust her after what happened in this room
You're a good girl trying to be honest
If you're not sorry I'll open up the ground under your feet and push you in

Prompt card 5: Brian's attitude to Irene
I can't hurt you because you're kind
I can't live with you now
Then you took the gun like all the rest
If I told anyone – and they couldn't understand – jeered – I wouldn't want to live not even with you

Prompt Card 6: Irene's new self-knowledge
Go to prison if you want but I have to live here
I thought the gun had bullets in it
It's your life. Do what you want. I'm not to blame.
I was – for a moment I understood. I did it
There was a child. It walked away. The little boy's dead.
Why? Let me live

There are many more references and quotations that you could use and, of course, all this could be used as the plan for a written character study.

Paths to production

The oppression of children by their parents is a theme Edward Bond wants us to explore. He is not asking children to go out and shoot their parents but he is asking us to think about the relationship between Irene and her father and to ask ourselves

what we think she should do, or rather what we would do in
similar circumstances.

Natalie Morse was at a state school in her final year of A-level
studies when she had to decide whether or not to take two
months off to play the part of Irene in *Tuesday*. She started
acting for fun when she was six and had gradually built up a
career alongside her ordinary school work, acting in adverts
and films.

> I was really excited when I was offered the part. I knew it
> would be a challenge but it was going to be a wonderful
> experience trying to come to terms with the problems of this
> sixteen-year-old. She was roughly my age and I believe
> what happened to her touches on the emotions of a lot of
> girls. Obviously it doesn't happen to everyone in the same
> way on one day but we have similar feelings and thoughts
> about authority and conflict and about the way you are
> prevented from doing what you know you can do.
>   Irene had been silenced by her father and had never
> questioned his authority. I think all fathers have some of this
> authoritarian streak. I have arguments with my dad because
> he thinks his opinion is correct and he doesn't listen, so I've
> had to assert myself. But Irene had been silenced for the
> whole of her life and suddenly this door opened for her. She
> knew what the right thing to do was. There was no
> compromise for her. I've never had to open such a difficult
> door in my life because my parents ultimately have let me
> make my decisions but I had to imagine what it would be
> like to be totally oppressed.
>   The interesting thing about *Tuesday* is the relationship
> between Irene and her father and I had to relate to both
> Edward and Bob in a kind of father/daughter relationship.
> Edward was very supportive and would always discuss a
> problem without giving too much away. With Bob it was a
> much closer feeling. The characters were very hostile to
> each other but off the set he was nurturing and supportive.
>   It was a very demanding and emotional part. It was very
> hard to go away at the end of a day's rehearsals. For two
> months I didn't know whether I was coming or going. I was

in an intensely dramatic situation and then I had to go home to my family and school friends and my A-level work. My parents will tell you I would come home emotionally drained and they had to take the brunt of it.

I didn't find it difficult to understand what Brian had been through. I understood that, when he talked about the boy in the desert walking away, Irene realised she could walk away herself. But the killing was another matter. I couldn't understand how a girl could kill her father and then one day Edward just told a story. He said it's like being in a lifeboat and he told the story. That was a revelation for me. It was so simple. The next day he had written the story down and from then on I had no problem with that critical scene. I understood that sometimes when you are in an unthinkable situation you have to do something which is unthinkable.

It was hard going back to school and examinations. It's not just coming to terms with the character, but the intensity of the experience. You have to know each other really well and rely on each other, so I do miss Edward and Ben and Bob, but in a deep sense Irene made me see things in different ways. She really opened my eyes to a lot of things. She is Edward's character but she will always be a part of me because of what I learned from her.

This is the story Edward Bond wrote for Natalie Morse to help her to understand more clearly some of the issues raised by the play.

The Plastic Water Bottle

A boat sank far out at sea. Six passengers survived in a lifeboat. Among them were a father and daughter. After drifting for three weeks the survivors had eaten their food. A plastic bottle of water was left.

They slept in shifts. Two survivors watched at all times. They kept watch in opposite directions. Between them they watched over the whole sea.

Each survivor took a sip of water at the beginning of each watch. Each drank six sips of water a day. They learnt that a sip may seem as large as an ocean measured in drops. Some of the survivors sipped longer than the others. They sipped with a deep intake that sounded like an angry hiss. Surely they were sipping more than their share?

The survivors were exhausted – on the margin of death. It was difficult to keep awake. They stood the plastic water bottle on the bench amidships. There it could be clearly seen.

Soon the plastic water bottle was half empty. One morning the girl feverishly drifted between sleeping and waking. The boat rocked. To her it seemed to be falling through space. Her limbs ached as if they were crushing her. She felt her mouth was like a metal funnel pushed into her face.

Her eyes opened a little. Her father was standing upright on the gunnel at the for'ard end of the boat. Half awake she wondered: why is father standing alone at the end of the boat? She saw that the bench amidships was empty. The plastic water bottle was in her father's hands. He had unscrewed the top and was raising the bottle to his lips. She realised he had gone to the end of the boat so that no one could stop him drinking. Had he been stealing the water – little by little for days? Was this the first time? The bottle had almost reached his lips.

Her eyes met her father's. She saw he was mad . . . she saw at once that he meant to gulp the water. His eyes glinted with dark spite. She knew that if he saw her raise the gun to shoot him he would throw the water into the sea. They would all die. But if she did not shoot him he would drink it and the rest of them would die even if he lived.

At the same moment she knew that she must shoot before he could drink the water or throw it into the sea. Yes now! She shot. The bullet went through the plastic water bottle. Two little jets shot out like a pair of horns. Wind was scattering the sparkling water. Her father was stunned. For a second he stared at the jets. Would he try to drink the water or throw it into the sea? She knew she must shoot him. The other survivors were waking up like shadows rising in the light.

She shot him three times. He fell into the boat. The bottle fell on top of him. Bouncing a little. She jumped forwards. Picked it up. Water sloshed from the end and trickled from the holes. It wetted her dead father's jacket. She stopped the holes with her fingers. The other survivors stared at her – some staring even from their sleep.

A third of the bottle still held water. It lasted the survivors more than a week. Then one died. They decided to watch one at a time. The watches would be shorter.

The Father in *Tuesday* was played by Bob Peck who has acted in several Bond plays over the past twenty years and played his Lear for two years in the Royal Shakespeare Company production at Stratford, the Barbican and on a continental tour. It was probably as a result of this that Edward Bond chose him for the part of Mr Briggs.

When Edward asked me to play the Father in *Tuesday* I wanted to do it for him, to work with him, because of the quality and challenge of the writing and because it was for schools. Edward had a very clear idea of what the Father should look like and encouraged me to act in ways for TV that I have guarded against in the past. He wanted a heightened performance, you might say a theatre perform- ance. In the past, when I've worked on Edward's plays, rehearsals would break down because we found the language impenetrable. We simply didn't know what the characters were trying to say or achieve. In a way I think he tries to make the characters say the unexpected. That doesn't mean he makes the characters inconsistent but it means you can never make any assumptions about any characters or their attitudes. They are shifting second by second and it makes you listen with complete attention. You can never drift off, either as an actor or as the audience.

When we were rehearsing *Tuesday* he would always try and get us to make decisions and make the exploration for ourselves. His very last resort would be to tell us what the meaning of something was.

The Father in *Tuesday* is a real character but he is not somebody you would meet on the street. He is a sort of distillation of a lot of people. To understand the character I try to bring my own experience to bear. I am a father and I recognise a lot of the man in myself. It's not just possessiveness – 'this is my house' – it's the temptation to use physical means and crude authority to get your offspring to do what you want instead of having a reasoned debate with them, treating them as equals, as human beings. This authoritarianism is very strong in parents and I think it is something this father has fallen prey to. It's the essence of his relationship with his daughter and in the play he's made to realise it's a sterile and dead relationship. In fact by the end he has no relationship and without it he is virtually dead. He's a walking corpse. All he has is his house.

It is a hard part to rehearse and play. We had more rehearsal before going into the studio for this than for any other TV play I have done and when we got into the studio we worked for twelve hours a day for over a week. They were very long days and it is very intense material: a man is held at the point of a gun by a young soldier he thinks is deranged, is made to go through a kind of mental torture and is shot at by his daughter. It is very highly charged and draining. When we were not actually on set recording, I would spend most of the time going over what was coming up, re-rehearsing in my head, rehearsing with the other actors or discussing with Edward what we should do. We would record a section of the play and then Edward would come down and give notes and try to move further on with an examination of the text. Even to the last take it was still work in progress.

Here are some lines which might focus your thinking about the father/daughter relationship.

You're not involving a girl her age. What sort of a father would I be if I encouraged you to do that.

Stay down there. I'm not playing about. I don't want you up here.

Am I supposed to lie in front of her? Your idea of a father.

No work. The house needs attention. I'd like to afford Irene a few extras.

If you look at me like that I'll put your eyes out. My God, I'm not a man of violence. I could take you outside and give you the thrashing of your life.

I'm answerable to no one in this house. What I do in this place is right
   because I say so.
I never rowed. We treated each other with respect.
If I was dead on the floor you'd be spitting on what was left.
Sometimes I'm not a good father. I lose my temper, rage. No job. I can't
   give you the authority of a father behind you. I tried to make up for
   my faults. I loved you.
Is this the return I get for a father's love?
In a way you've set me free. Now there's nothing to pretend. We must go
   on. I have to live with you.
I need you to tell me . . . I've been like this for years.

The father/daughter relationship is one theme in the play
which you can talk and write about to help you understand the
play and your own relationships.

- Hot-seat the Father and question him about his life and his
  relationship to his daughter
- Prepare a debate on the motion: By and large, parents do
  more good than harm
- Write an account, real or imagined, of a relationship
  between a parent and a teenager

Now make a similar study of another theme in *Tuesday* and
treat it in the same way.

Every word you choose, every phrase you use: the drafting process

On 17 August 1992 Edward Bond wrote an outline of the play
he was going to write:

Teenage girl (*A*) has boyfriend in army (*S*). He's at war
(Gulf, N. Ireland, Falklands or in some other colonial war).
   He comes back having deserted: because of seeing
soldiers killing – they'd said they'd joined in order to kill but
hadn't thought about it – said same sort of thing himself etc.
Describes incident to girl. Wants her to put him up for a
while. Doesn't want to go on the run.
   A's father (*F*) returns. Knows S has deserted? (local

radio?) – argument – that S must do his duty – he's going to denounce S.

S: Where's he going?

A: Downstairs to phone.

S pulls gun on F – will kill him. Argument moves to more profound level. S couldn't kill him – not unless it's to save his own neck – kill someone rather than to go to gaol for a few years etc. Hypocrite.

A: You don't have to interfere etc. – don't have to know he's here.

F: Duty.

A: Both stop it.

Tells S to give her the gun. A follows S down. She pleads with F that he'll destroy her relationship, she'll never forgive him etc. F more determined. Won't phone – instead going to the police station immediately. F goes to door.

A aims at F. Pulls trigger. Click – gun not loaded.

F: You tried to kill me!

Shocked silence. F comes towards A. Stops. Click. Click. Click – she frantically tries to shoot F.

F: You're mad.

S could come in – he's been watching through the door? Waiting upstairs??

Leads to reconsideration of situation. All F can do is say: She tried to shoot me. S insists that weapons etc. change situations – that people find themselves doing terrible things before they know it etc.

F: Why did you try to shoot me?

A: I don't know.

F: But she meant it. She meant it. She tried to again – kept trying.

Could mother enter here?

S says here or later that he'd never put a bullet in because he'd never, never kill anyone.

F: Well your girlfriend would.

When S hears mother's voice he disappears rapidly back to A's room. Later she goes to kiss or hold him: he won't have anything to do with her because she's a killer.

Go through the first part of *Tuesday* and compare it to Edward

Bond's synopsis. Work out what has been retained and what has been left out. Can you think of reasons for the changes?

Once the writing starts there is an evolution from a first idea, through many drafts, to the finished text.

What follows is an example of how Edward Bond worked on one tiny but crucial description. It is well worth studying how the language is changed and shaped: what is kept from the start; ideas that are dropped; the slight change in order to give a change of emphasis; the way the language is pared down and simplified so that the scene which is being described comes into sharp focus like a black and white photograph.

Get five different people to rehearse the different versions. Try to evaluate the dramatic significance of the changes that Edward Bond made and then make a presentation of the five versions giving a commentary explaining what you have found out.

VERSION 1

It was in the desert. We were quiet ourselves. The raids were still going on. You could see them flying over. We were quiet waiting for the order to go in a few days. They said stand down. The padre was singing hymns in his tent. I went for a walk. You can do that – slip away. You could even walk into no-man's-land. It was all our land really. Great big beefburger we're just waiting to put our teeth in. (*Sighs.*) I'm trying to tell you. It isn't much. I was in the sand. Dunes – little waves cut in them by the sea. Very regular, beautiful. Then here and there it's slashed open by a tank. A bloody great big steel machine dragging its grave round behind it. Little men hiding in the nets – camouflage. Ripped the dunes open – as if you could punch holes in the sea. And then it was flat. All those little bits of sand. Rock once. Little bits of silver grit. And then over there – quite a way off – I saw a bundle. It was white but dark. Gleaming and moving. I thought a mirage. But in war everything is unreal. You don't know what anything is any more. Unless you've got an order you shoot it or squash it. Then I thought, a little dwarf or a fat periscope under the sand.

VERSION 2

In the desert. Quiet. The planes were still raiding. See them
going over. It made the desert quieter. We were waiting for
the order to go in. Take a few days. Temporary stand by. I
went for a walk. You can slip away though it's war. Into no-
man's-land. I haven't got much to tell you. Don't expect
much. Sand dunes. Little waves on their sides. Regular.
Really beautiful. Then where the tanks had slashed them
open. Steel machines dragging their graves round with
them. Then I crossed that and came to where it was still and
flat. Flatter than the sky. All that sand. And I saw – some
way off, I don't know how far? – a shadow moving. Black
dot. I didn't see that thing above it that made the shadow.
At first it was white – lost in the glare. Then I saw it was
something walking in its own shadow as if that was a puddle.
A mirage. In war you're part of a mirage. Or a periscope
sticking up from the sand. I went closer. It was walking. A
man. A dwarf.

VERSION 3

In the desert, in the quiet. Waiting for the order to go in.
Temporary wait for a few days. Sitting. You can slip away
even in war. Into no-man's-land. I went for a walk. I haven't
got much to tell. I don't know if I can make you understand
the sand. Little waves on the dunes. Regular, beautiful.
Then the trenches where tanks had slashed them open.
Machines dragging graves round behind them. Then I came
to the still and flat sand. Flatter than the sky. I saw – some
way off, how far? – a shadow moving. Black dot. At first I
didn't see the thing above that made the dot. It was lost in
the heat. Then I saw something white was walking in its own
shadow. A mirage. In war you're in a mirage. A periscope
sticking up from a dugout?

VERSION 4

It happened in the desert. Temporary hold-up. A few days'
quiet before the order to go in. Even in war you can slip
away. It's not much of a story. I went for a walk in no-
man's-land. Over the dunes . . . covered in long rows of neat
little waves. Beautiful. Then where they're slashed open by

tanks. Machines dragging their graves behind them. I went on. It was still. Flat sand, flatter than the sky. I saw – how far off? – a shadow moving. Black. Dot. First I didn't see the thing that made the shadow. It was lost in heat. Then I saw something white walking. A mirage? In war you're in a mirage. A periscope sticking up from a buried dugout? I got closer. Still walking. A man. A dwarf.

VERSION 5

It's not much of a story. It was in the desert. A temporary hold-up. A few days' quiet before the order to go in. Even in war you can slip away. I took a walk in no-man's-land. The dunes. Covered in long neat rows of little waves. Beautiful. Then where they'd been slashed open by tanks. Machines dragging their graves behind them. Went on. It was still. Flat. Sand. Flatter than the sky. I saw – how far? – a shadow. Black. Dot. A periscope sticking up from a buried dugout? No it was a moving shadow. First I didn't see the thing that made it. Lost in the heat. Then I saw something white. Walking on the shadow. A mirage? In war you're in a mirage. I got closer. A man. A dwarf. Walking in its own shadow.

Ideas for writing

One of the skills in talking and writing about a play is to refer to things that happen (references) and to quote what characters say (quotations). You must be able to use quotations and references to back up anything you say.

Some quotations can be used to illustrate more than one point.

FATHER. *Oh it's you. I thought it was her other one.*

The quotation could be used as evidence that Brian was not all that special to Irene since she was going out with more than one boy; or that Irene was, to use her father's words, '*a pathetic little tart*', or that Brian was special to Irene and her father was trying to make a cruel and petty joke.

Look at the following quotations. Decide who is speaking

and what the circumstances are. Work out how the quotations could be used to support more than one point of view.

- *My father hides his money in his room. I'll steal it.*
- *Us or them. You look after your own. Thank God I've got Rene to care for.*
- *You're a considerate lad. Good at heart. That's why Rene took you up.*

Try to use short quotations and indicate either before or after the quotation why you have used it. Here is an example of how to use a reference and a quotation with an explanation.

I won't forget the child.
I went for the wrong walk.
I met myself.

This line expresses an idea that is central to *Tuesday*. The image of the child is seared into Brian's memory. He can hardly bear to speak about it but when he does he gives a precise and beautiful description. He sees himself as the child walking away from the oppressive authority of the family and state. And yet, at the same time, he sees the child growing up 'into one of theirs to kill us' or being found as 'a little skeleton with sand in its mouth'.

Notice how the quotation is put on a separate line. There is no rule that says this must be so but it makes it easier to read the text. It also means that you do not need to use quotation marks. A useful rule-of-thumb is: if the quotation is only two or three words let it appear as part of your sentence using quotation marks; otherwise put it on a separate line.

After Irene has tried to shoot her father, Brian says:

I'm like him. I can't live with you now.

In other words, by showing she is capable of killing, Irene has become like all the other killers that sicken Brian.

If you write about any of the following always base your ideas firmly on the text of *Tuesday*. Where appropriate use references and quotations and always use your writing to help you reflect on Edward Bond's ideas.

- The inquest into the death of Brian
- An interview with Irene at the age of 80
- Imagine the death of Brian is not seen on stage but is recounted by Irene or the Father. Write one of the speeches
- Imagine the death of the soldier is seen on stage. Write the stage directions and dialogue
- Write a story based on the idea of the whole world being turned upside down by one unexpected event
- Write an extra scene showing the incident when Brian left the barracks

Just when you thought you had finished . . .

In a letter written after *Tuesday* was broadcast Edward Bond wrote about his concern that students should not concentrate only on the characters in *Tuesday*:

> It would be useful to direct attention to the relationship between the room and the desert and the relationship between state authority and family authority.

He goes on to ask a series of questions:

> Why does Irene feel it necessary to shoot her father? Why does the soldier carry an unloaded gun? Why does the soldier who has already killed say he will never kill? In what way is the girl with the gun different from the soldier with the bayonet? Is there a contradiction between the father's attitude to the bayoneting of the soldier and his reaction to his daughter's attempt to kill him? What is the play trying to make us experience and think about?

He concludes by saying:

> I feel the play should help students to put their own immediate personal relationships into a wider context and to see how external authority uses private lives for its own ends. Irene discovers this and changes her life by making a stand against it. Otherwise protest becomes a matter of wearing too much make-up or having the 'wrong' sort of haircut. This trivialises protest and really is setting up a false quarrel with authority. It changes little.

Methuen Modern Plays

include work by

Jean Anouilh
John Arden
Margaretta D'Arcy
Peter Barnes
Sebastian Barry
Brendan Behan
Edward Bond
Bertolt Brecht
Howard Brenton
Simon Burke
Jim Cartwright
Caryl Churchill
Noël Coward
Sarah Daniels
Nick Dear
Shelagh Delaney
David Edgar
Dario Fo
Michael Frayn
John Godber
Paul Godfrey
David Greig
John Guare
Peter Handke
Jonathan Harvey
Iain Heggie
Declan Hughes
Terry Johnson
Sarah Kane
Charlotte Keatley
Barrie Keeffe
Robert Lepage
Stephen Lowe

Doug Lucie
Martin McDonagh
John McGrath
David Mamet
Patrick Marber
Arthur Miller
Mtwa, Ngema & Simon
Tom Murphy
Phyllis Nagy
Peter Nichols
Joseph O'Connor
Joe Orton
Louise Page
Joe Penhall
Luigi Pirandello
Stephen Poliakoff
Franca Rame
Mark Ravenhill
Philip Ridley
Reginald Rose
David Rudkin
Willy Russell
Jean-Paul Sartre
Sam Shepard
Wole Soyinka
C. P. Taylor
Theatre de Complicite
Theatre Workshop
Sue Townsend
Judy Upton
Timberlake Wertenbaker
Victoria Wood

Methuen World Classics *and*
Methuen Contemporary Dramatists

Aeschylus (two volumes)

Jean Anouilh

John Arden (two volumes)

Arden & D'Arcy

Aristophanes (two volumes)

Aristophanes & Menander

Peter Barnes (three volumes)

Sebastian Barry

Brendan Behan

Aphra Behn

Edward Bond (five volumes)

Bertolt Brecht (six volumes)

Howard Brenton (two volumes)

Büchner

Bulgakov

Calderón

Jim Cartwright

Anton Chekhov

Caryl Churchill (two volumes)

Noël Coward (five volumes)

Sarah Daniels (two volumes)

Eduardo De Filippo

David Edgar (three volumes)

Euripides (three volumes)

Dario Fo (two volumes)

Michael Frayn (two volumes)

Max Frisch

Gorky

Harley Granville Barker
   (two volumes)

Peter Handke

Henrik Ibsen (six volumes)

Terry Johnson

Bernard-Marie Koltès

Lorca (three volumes)

David Mamet (three volumes)

Marivaux

Mustapha Matura

David Mercer (two volumes)

Arthur Miller (five volumes)

Anthony Minghella (two volumes)

Molière

Tom Murphy (four volumes)

Musset

Peter Nichols (two volumes)

Clifford Odets

Joe Orton

Philip Osment

Louise Page

A. W. Pinero

Luigi Pirandello

Stephen Poliakoff (two volumes)

Terence Rattigan

Christina Reid

Willy Russell

Ntozake Shange

Sam Shepard (two volumes)

Sophocles (two volumes)

Wole Soyinka

David Storey (two volumes)

August Strindberg (three volumes)

J. M. Synge

Sue Townsend

Ramón del Valle-Inclán

Frank Wedekind

Michael Wilcox

Oscar Wilde

For a Complete Catalogue of Methuen Drama titles
write to:

Methuen Drama
Random House
20 Vauxhall Bridge Road
London SW1V 2SA